Discipline
and Classroom Control

Discipline
and Classroom Control

A Special
Interest Resource Guide
in Education

Compiled by Sara Lake

ORYX PRESS

The rare Arabian Oryx, a desert antelope dating from Biblical times, is believed to be the prototype of the mythical unicorn. The World Wildlife Fund found three of the animals in 1962, and aware that they were nearing extinction, sent them to the Phoenix Zoo as the nucleus of a breeding herd in captivity. Today the Oryx population is nearing 200 and herds have been returned to breeding grounds in Israel and Jordan.

Copyright © 1980 by The Oryx Press
2214 N. Central at Encanto
Phoenix, AZ 85004

Published simultaneously in Canada

Printed and Bound in the United States of America

Library of Congress Cataloging in Publication Data

Lake, Sara.
    Discipline and classroom control.

    Includes index.
    1. Classroom management.   2. School discipline.
I. Title.
LB3013.L28   016.3715   80-19462

ISBN 0-912700-71-8

Contents

Introduction

It is the intent of this guide to present a broad overview of the literature on school discipline, covering the material published in the period from 1975 through autumn 1979. While the emphasis is on practical techniques and programs useful to school-site personnel, research and evaluative studies have been included selectively. Most of the documents cited are addressed to regular class teachers and principals in elementary and secondary schools, but there are also citations of specific interest to special education teachers, counselors, vocational teachers, community groups, and others interested in this issue.

These citations were compiled from computer searches of six databases: ERIC, Psychological Abstracts, Comprehansive Dissertation Index,* Social Sci-Search, Sociological Abstracts, and Magazine Index, as well as from manual searches of Education Index and the extensive professional library and information files of the San Mateo Educational Resources Center (SMERC).

The guide is divided into four sections, some of which have subsections:

Section I consists mainly of research studies and theoretical discussions, and provides an overview of the discipline "crisis": an historical perspective; statistics on the incidence of discipline problems; attitude surveys of school and community groups; and analysis of some contributing factors and variables in student misbehavior and school control.

Section II presents descriptions and evaluations of specific disciplinary programs and/or practices. The initial subsection includes surveys of existing school practices and studies attempting to pinpoint the most effective student management techniques. The next three subsections present literature on the pros and cons of three of the most controversial disciplinary methods in use: corporal punishment, suspension/expulsion, and behavior modification. The final subsection of this chapter concerns alternative programs and techniques, including, but not limited to: inschool suspension, student participation models, and the teacher-centered programs of Canter (Assertive Discipline), Gordon (Teacher Effectiveness Training), and Glasser.

Section III is addressed to elementary and secondary level teachers and extends practical advice and guidelines for general classroom management and for dealing with specific behavior problems. Some inservice packages are cited.

Section IV concerns school-level disciplinary methods. It is chiefly intended for the building principal and counseling staff. Because court litigation has had such an impact on school discipline practices in recent years, the first subsection examines legal issues and the definition of due process in student disciplinary cases. The second subsection provides philosophical statements, guidelines, and model policies on the governance of students.

Within each subsection, citations are arranged by document format: journal articles, microfiche documents, and books. Notation is made on those citations known to be available for purchase from a standard source. On selected journal articles, the notation "Reprint: UMI" indicates that a photocopy of the article may be purchased from:

Article Copy Service-CIJE
University Microfilms International
300 North Zeeb Road
Ann Arbor, MI 48106
(800) 521-3042

---

*The dissertation titles and abstracts from this database are published with permission of University Microfilms International, publishers of *Dissertation Abstracts International* (Copyright © 1980 by University Microfilms International), and may not be reproduced without their prior permission. These abstracts are indicated throughout this Resource Guide by an asterisk after the title.

All cited microfiche documents have order codes and source acronyms, indicating their availability from one of three ordering sources, as listed below:

DC   University Microfilms
          Dissertation Copies
          P.O. Box 1764
          Ann Arbor, MI 48106
          (800) 521-3042

EDRS   ERIC Document Reproduction Service
          P.O. Box 190
          Arlington, VA 22210
          (703) 841-1212

SMERC San Mateo Educational Resources Center
          333 Main Street
          Redwood City, CA 94063
          (415) 364-5600 ext 4403

Overview: The Discipline Crisis

Statistics, Trends, Perceptions

JOURNAL ARTICLES

1. **Are Students Behaving Worse than They Used to Behave?** Doyle, Walter. *Journal of Research and Development in Education.* v11, n4, p3–16, Sum 1978 (EJ 189 887; Reprint: UMI).

   The emphasis of this article is on students and the evolving character of their affiliations with schooling. It compares school conditions of the 1890s with those of 1970s, and presents a brief and selective review of professional literature on school discipline published during this 80-year span.

2. **Destructive Norm-Violating School Behavior among Adolescents: A Review of Protective and Preventive Efforts.** Sabatino, David A. et al. *Adolescence.* v13, n52, p675–86, Win 1978 (EJ 202 612; Reprint: UMI).

   This article reviews statistics on the growth of vandalism and personal violence by secondary school students; suggests possible causes and motives; and describes programs designed to reduce and prevent the incidence in the nation's schools.

3. **Discipline in the Public Schools: A Problem of Perception?** Williams, John W. *Phi Delta Kappan.* v60, n5, p385–87, Jan 1979 (EJ 193 990; Reprint: UMI).

   After examining the results of polls and other indicators of attitudes toward discipline in the schools, the author concludes that our perception of the problem has not changed significantly in 25 years and that the solution, self-responsibility, is the same now as then.

4. **Discipline Problems in Georgia Secondary Schools —1961 and 1974.** Kingston, Albert J.; Gentry, Harold W. *NASSP Bulletin.* v61, n406, p94–99, Feb 1977.

   Compares data on discipline problems in Georgia secondary schools that were gathered in similar surveys of secondary school principals in 1961 and 1974.

5. **The Eleventh Annual Gallup Poll of the Public's Attitudes toward the Public Schools.** Gallup, George H. *Phi Delta Kappan.* v61, n1, p33–45, Sep 1979.

   This 1979 survey again finds that the public perceives the perennial problem of discipline as the most important problem facing the public schools. Data on public perceptions of school problems, educational costs, and improvement methods are provided.

6. **How Administrators View the Crisis in School Discipline.** Duke, Daniel L. *Phi Delta Kappan.* v59, n5, p325–30, Jan 1978 (EJ 169 845; Reprint: UMI).

   School administrators in California and New York share views on what are the most pressing discipline problems— skipping class, truancy, and tardiness—but those views do not seem to be shared by teachers and students. The administrators are taking steps to resolve the problems.

7. **The Safe School Study Report to the Congress: Evaluation and Recommendations—A Summary of Testimony to the House Education and Labor Subcommittee on Economic Opportunity.** Emrich, Robert L. *Crime and Delinquency.* v24, n3, p266–76, Jul 1978 (EJ 184 603; Reprint: UMI).

   Presents a critique of the HEW Safe School Study Report, including various methodological problems. Suggests that only the broad findings are trustworthy and recommends specific legislation designed to combat the vandalism problem.

8. **School Discipline: Yesterday, Today, and Tomorrow.** Hart, James E.; Lordon, John F. *Clearing House.* v52, n2, p68–71, Oct 1978.

   The author explains the evolving nature of discipline problems, the dilemmas of today's educator in dealing with discipline, and offers suggestions for developing a positive classroom atmosphere and positive discipline policies, based on reasonable and just rules.

9. School Discipline and Corporal Punishment: An American Retrospect. Raichle, Donald R. *Interchange*. v8, p1–2, 71–83, 1977–78 (EJ 176 435; Reprint: UMI).

The author presents a retrospective examination of the recurring conflict between the inculcation of America's cultural heritage and the development of the child as a free individual, by examining the concept of "school discipline" as practiced from colonial days through the twentieth century.

10. Silent Classrooms in Violent Schools. Ruchkin, Judith P. *Action in Teacher Education*. v1, n2, p61–65, Fall-Win 1978 (EJ 197 178; Reprint: UMI).

This study of school violence presents data establishing the extent of deviant behavior, a theory explaining deviance in the schools, and some policy variables.

11. What Happened to the High School Discipline Crisis? Duke, Daniel Linden; Perry, Cheryl. *Urban Education*. v14, n2, p182–204, Jul 1979.

Fifty-one percent of the principals of California high schools responded to a mail survey about the number of discipline problems, illegal absences, and suspensions in their schools, and their perceptions of the seriousness of the discipline problem. In contrast to recent writings about a discipline 'crisis', this study found that only 4 percent of the respondents felt that their schools faced major problems. Quantitative data suggested that the great majority of California students are attending school regularly and behaving appropriately. The technical problems of this and other discipline studies are considered at length.

REPORTS

12. An Analysis of Class Period Truancy in the High Schools.* Jackson, Horace David, United States International University, 1976, 180p (76–22, 386; Reprint: DC).

The problem of this study was to ascertain why large numbers of students come to high school on a regular basis, attend some classes, and, without authorization, absent themselves from others.

The heart of the study lies in its attempt to answer ten broad questions relating to period truancy in the high schools of the Riverside Unified School District. In order to collect data to answer these questions, the researcher developed three inventories which were administered to a random sample of period truants and nontruants to secure additional information.

In order to obtain additional statistical information the writer surveyed 87 truant students and 88 nontruant students.

The students were asked to respond to 35 questions, which were clustered around the four areas listed below:(1)The truant's and nontruant's responses to their perceptions of the curriculum.(2) The perception of the truants and nontruants of preventive measures for period truancy.(3) The responses of the truant and nontruant regarding their perception of the staff's expectations.(4)The responses of the truant and non-truant regarding their families' attitudes and expectations.

The t-T was applied to responses to the four cluster areas previously described.

There was a significant difference in three of the areas of comparison between the truant and the nontruant. In the area of staff expectation, there was no significant difference between the truant and the nontruant.

Additional information obtained from the interviewing of students, parents, and teachers indicates the following: The Period Truant (1) tends to read two or three years below grade level, (2) is not involved in extra-curricular activities, (3) is often influenced by friends to remain out of class, (4) is bored with most of the materials presented, (5) is often involved in personal problems that are not related to the school. The Nontruant (1) will attend class, may be bored with the materials being presented, (2) is often involved in extra-curricular activities, (3) is usually successful in school, (4) is usually supported by his parents, (5) is able to do long-range planning.

From the results four main conclusions were drawn. These are as follows: (1) The parents, the student, the school, and the community all contribute to period truancy. (2) The high school curriculum has not been able to maintain its relevancy in such a rapid changing society. (3) The inability of students to find success in a given class in school is a contributing factor to period truancy. (4) The deterioration of the family unit is a contributing factor to period truancy.

13. Analysis of Hawaii Secondary School Discipline Variables. Kalus, Janet Marie Wolcott. Dec 1978, 288p; Ph.D. Dissertation, Walden University (ED 170 868; Reprint: EDRS).

It was the intent of this study to examine student discipline problems in 21 high schools on the island of Oahu in Hawaii. Literature was reviewed concerning the youth revolution as it affects students in Hawaiian public schools and concerning discipline problems unique to them. Data were collected through a questionnaire administered to selected students, teachers, and school administrators. Principals reported truancy as the most frequently occurring problem. Burglary, vandalism, smoking, and drug use were marked by most principals as occurring either "frequently" or "occasionally." Fighting and disorderly conduct occurred with moderate frequency. Principals reported eight teachers had been assaulted by students in the past year. Brush fires and fires in trash receptacles were problems in almost half the schools. More than half the principals reported arson at their schools in the past year. It was established that a school's enrollment size is positively correlated with crime rate. No association was found between school-community relations and crime rate.

A correlation was established between high parental interest in school and low crime rate. Twelve recommendations were suggested, including that principals ought to have high academic and behavior expectations for the school.

14. A Comparison of Child Behavior Related Discipline Problems of Secondary and Elementary School Educators of Louisiana.* Connella, William Eugene, Northwestern State University of Louisiana, 1975, 172p (75–27, 500; Reprint: DC).

The purpose of this study was to determine the significant differences that exist in the responses of secondary and elementary educators in Louisiana on the selection of discipline measures in the following categories: punitive measures, moralizing, medical referral, individualized work, praise or encouragement, and observation of the child for cause of behavior.

A field study was used to collect data from 300 educators randomly selected from the state of Louisiana. Included in the sample were 48 counselors, 162 teachers, and 50 principals.

The criterion instrument used for the collection of the data was the *Modified Stendler Survey*, which presented 25 child behavior related discipline problems with 6 discipline responses.

The Chi square statistic was used at the .05 level of significance to determine if differences exist between the educators' responses to the various categories.

Conclusions drawns from this study were:

1. The level of the educator as a composite group, elementary or secondary, has a statistically significant influence on the choice of disciplinary measure selected to deal with child behavior related discipline problems.

2. The position of the teacher, elementary or secondary, has no significant influence on the choice of disciplinary measures that are selected to handle child behavior related discipline problems.

3. The position of the counselor, elementary or secondary, has no significant influence on the choice of disciplinary measure selected to deal with child behavior related discipline problems.

4. The position of the principals, elementary and secondary, has no significant influence on the selection of disciplinary measure chosen to administer child behavior related discipline problems.

5. The sex of the educator, male or female, has a significant influence on the response of disciplinary measures selected to deal with child behavior related discipline problems.

6. The experience level of educators has significant influence on the choice of disciplinary measure selected to handle child behavior related discipline problems as indicated by the lower percent of nontenured teachers for the correct action response.

7. The race of an educator, Black or White, has significant influence on the choice of disciplinary measures that are selected to deal with child behavior discipline problems.

15. A Comparison of Perceptions of School Discipline between Students, Parents, Teachers, and School Administrators.* Rice, Robert C., Iowa State University, 1977, 213p (77-29, 863; Reprint: DC).

This study dealt with ascertaining perceptions about discipline held by administrators, teachers, students, and students' parents.

Parents, students, teachers, and administrators were asked to identify the five most crucial discipline problems facing public schools in their community. An array of problems was provided from which respondents could choose and space was provided for open-ended input. The data revealed the following: (1) Most often perceived problems were: (a) pupils' lack of interest, (b) finances, (c) discipline, (d) curriculum, and (e) parents' lack of interest. (2) The majority of students perceived "pupils' lack of interest" as important; however, few administrators agreed. (3) Over three-fourths of the eastern sample believed "finances" was a major problem, a belief that less than half of the remaining sample held.

Most significant differences were generated by responses as to whether discipline was "not strict enough" and "about right." (1) Seven of ten teachers and respondents over 30 identified discipline as a major problem. (2) Six of ten administrators, students, and those under 30 did not perceive discipline as a major problem. (3) Southern and western respondents agreed with teachers and parents, while northern and eastern respondents were evenly divided. (4) While administrators viewed truancy and tardiness as most serious, parents selected smoking, drugs, and alcohol.

This study revealed one major difference compared to the last seven Gallup Polls of Attitudes on Public Education, i.e., many respondents perceived "pupils' lack of interest" as the most serious problem. Respondents also chose "teaching students how to solve problems and think for themselves" as first choice among six alternatives for reducing discipline problems.

16. Conflict and Change: The School as Reality. Diem, Richard A. Nov 1976, 12p; Paper presented at the Annual Meeting of the National Council for the Social Studies (Washington, DC, November 4–7, 1976) (ED 134 506; Reprint: EDRS; also available from: Richard A. Diem, Division of Education, University of Texas, San Antonio, TX 78285).

An examination of rules and regulations of five schools within a 15-mile radius in Cook County, Illinois, illustrates the diverse nature of behavior problems in schools. Overcrowding, race, poverty, and drugs are suggested by social scientists to be among the causes for disruptions within school systems. The schools in this study include an entirely Black inner-city school; a multicultural, economically diverse school in an old established suburban community; a private parochial school with tuition of $1,900 per year; a school with students from predominantly upper and middle income classes; and a school which serves five culturally different suburbs. A comparison of guidelines for student behavior as codified in student handbooks is made. Punishable infractions range from excessive absences to abuses of property rights and use of dangerous drugs or illegal substances, i.e., guns and knives. Each school has different policies dealing with infractions: the private school institutes immediate expulsion for serious first offenses, whereas other schools hold conferences between school personnel and parents before expelling unruly students. The author points out that adolescents commit more crime per capita than any other age group. He urges that society as a whole must deal with problems of violence in order for the school to overcome discipline problems.

17. Crime and Punishment in the Schooling Process: A Historical Analysis. Newman, Joan; Newman, Graeme, National Council on Crime and Delinquency, Hackensack, NJ, NewGate Resource Center, Feb 1978, 35p; Chapter 24 of "Theoretical Perspectives on School Crime, Volume I." Sponsoring agency: Department of Health, Education, and Welfare, Washington, DC (ED 157 192; Reprint: EDRS).

One of 52 theoretical papers on school crime and its relation to poverty, this chapter examines the historical validity of two popular beliefs concerning the "crisis of discipline" in schools. One is that it is something special to this turbulent age, and the other is that school violence and crime have increased because we have relaxed our discipline. The authors conclude that, while it is probable that school violence and crime have increased in this century, the increase is not sufficient to warrant the conclusion that it has resulted from the relaxation of discipline. Until this century, schools have traditionally been places of violence—where teachers severely corporally punished their students, and where students frequently rose up in rebellion, riots, and mutinies. In comparison, this century has seen an incredible delimiting of severe corporal punishment (although it is still widely used), which has not been matched with an equally severe increase in school violence.

18. Crime in North Carolina Schools: The Perception and Response of Administrators.* Harlan, John Paxon, Jr., The University of North Carolina at Greensboro, 1979, 380p (79-22 410; Reprint: DC).

The purpose of this study was to examine the perception of school-related crime by public school superintendents within the State of North Carolina and to examine their administrative reaction to those perceptions. The respondents were queried by means of a prevalidated survey instrument which was mailed to each respondent.

Based on the responses to the survey, it can be concluded that administrators perceive crime (at least crimes against the school plant) as a problem within the schools. Moreover, 54 percent of the respondents reported that their districts have a "policy" on the reporting of "all offenses" to both the central office and to the police. Conversely, only 25 percent of the respondents reported they had a similar "policy" for reporting offenses against school personnel to both the central office and the police. Therefore, one can conclude that administrators perceive a crime problem and this problem was predominately seen as a problem of offenses against the school plant.

The principal reaction by the respondents to the perceived problem was primarily the formulation of a policy on the reporting of crimes against the school plant. Only 10 percent of the respondents reported the establishment of a security unit within their districts. In addition, one district reported that a security unit was in the formation stage. Conversely, 88 percent of the respondents reported that they had no security unit. Further, there was no additional evidence of any interest in this type of response.

19. Discipline Study. Finnegan, Harry, Spokane School District 81, WA, Apr 1976, 57p (ED 122 450; Reprint: EDRS).

A questionnaire was used to help define student discipline, categorize and rank the concerns of different groups regarding student discipline, and provide examples of issues. The questionnaire asked citizens, parents, students, teachers, counselors, and principals to list the most important, second most important, and third most important problems regarding discipline and to provide examples of each problem. The results of the survey are presented by educational level—elementary, junior high, and senior high. Two charts are provided with each set of results. One chart ranks the top eight concerns of each group, and the other displays the frequency with which the major categories were cited by the five groups surveyed. The 16 categories the responses fell into are attendance; class size; discipline (control and supervision); discrimination; external influence; lack of parental guidance; lack of respect; miscellaneous; parent-teacher cooperation; physical abuse; rights and responsibilities (legal); smoking, drugs, and alcohol; staff behavior; student attitude; too much freedom; and vandalism and theft.

20. The Extent of High School Truancy and Profiles of Truants and Nontruants.* Kowalski, Ken Croydon, University of Virginia, 1975, 97p (76-1086; Reprint: DC).

The basic purposes of this study were to determine the extent of truancy by grade level and by size of school in urban, suburban, and other high schools in Virginia; to develop profiles of the truant and the nontruant based on information available in school records; and to compare the profile of the truant with that of the nontruant.

Data were collected from each high school in Virginia concerning the number of students, by grade level, who had been absent at least 20 percent of their days in membership during the 1973–74 school year. Data were analyzed according to the classifications of urban, suburban, and other; and large and small schools.

To obtain data concerning the characteristics of truants, and nontruants for purposes of comparison, a systematic sample of 120 truant and 120 nontruant students was obtained from a sample of 12 schools. Information was sought through an instrument designed to be completed by a counselor or other school official.

The means of the truancy rates among the grade levels were very similar, ranging from 9.1 percent to 9.7 percent. There was, however, wide variation within and among the schools, ranging from no truancy to more than 40 percent truancy for a particular grade within one school. Generally, urban schools were found to have truancy rates significantly higher than those of either suburban or other schools. There were no statistically significant differences in the mean truancy rates between small and large schools; however, there was a tendency towards lower rates in small schools.

Truants tended to have lower IQ scores, poorer grades, and lower standardized achievement test scores than did nontruants. Truants tended to participate in school activities less frequently than did nontruants. Family income for truants tended to be less than for nontruants. Parents of truants tended to be employed in less skilled jobs than parents of nontruants, and also tended to have less formal education. The number of parents at home was the same for both truants and nontruants. Although not statistically significant, truants more often than nontruants came from large families.

21. Failing Students—Failing Schools: A Study of Dropouts and Discipline in New York State.

Block, Eve E. et al., New York Civil Liberties Union, Apr 1978, 215p; not available in hard copy due to reproduction quality of original document (ED 160 674; Reprint: EDRS; also available from Statewide Youth Advocacy Project, 429 Powers Building, Rochester, NY 14614).

This report focuses on underschooling in the state of New York. The study provides statistics on dropouts, examines students' reasons for leaving school, and analyzes the school histories of dropouts with respect to patterns of disruption, truancy, and academic failure. Suggestions of school administrators and dropouts on how students might be encouraged to remain in school are presented. Pupil achievement and compensatory education programs are also considered. The study hypothesizes a relationship between dropping out, prior school disciplinary problems, and academic inadequacy. Based on data from interviews, individual school districts, and central agency statistics, it is concluded that (1) the state does not provide appropriate education for over 500,000 students; (2) school disciplinary policies are seldom made public and are not clear; (3) students over 16 are frequently illegally excluded from school; (4) few schools provide a climate conducive to individualized education; and (5) the state education department does not adequately monitor the indices of school problems.

22. General Report of the Alberta School Discipline Study, 1975–76.

Alberta University, Edmonton, Apr 1977, 222p. Sponsoring agency: Alberta Department of Education, Edmonton; Alberta School Trustees' Association, Edmonton; Alberta Teachers Association, Edmonton (ED 140 454; Reprint: EDRS).

This study originated as a result of public concern about standards of behavior. The purposes of the study were to ascertain what school discipline was in fact like and what it should be like, and to provide information to practitioners. An extensive review of the literature was conducted. Nine groups—principals, vice-principals, teachers, students, parents, superintendents, central office personnel, trustees, and regional office personnel—were surveyed. The reaction of the largest single group, a plurality of 41 percent of all participants, was that school discipline as it was in 1975–76 was just about right. Parents especially endorsed this view, while trustees and teachers especially endorsed the second most popular view that discipline was a little lenient. Although groups differed one from another in their views, group differences were overshadowed by the diversity of views within any one group. The study found little difference in views on school discipline between participants associated with different grade levels and some difference between participants associated with urban and rural schools. Participants felt that large elementary schools were associated with discipline problems.

23. Neither Corporal Punishment Cruel nor Due Process Due: The United States Supreme Court's Decision in "Ingraham v. Wright."

Piele, Philip K. Jul 1977, 36p; Paper presented at the East-West Culture Learning Institute's Seminar on "Problems of Law and Society: Asia, the Pacific, and the United States" (Honolulu, HI, July 25–August 25, 1977) (ED 145 535; Reprint: EDRS).

This paper examines some of the historical and contemporary assumptions regarding the social and educational context of the use of corporal punishment on children, assumptions that are implicit in the Supreme Court's decision in the Ingraham v. Wright case. Beginning with a summary of the Florida case, the author outlines the Court's majority opinion concerning the constitutional issues (involving the Eighth and Fourteenth Amendments), and the dissenting minority's positions. The majority held that corporal punishment of school children neither constitutes "cruel and unusual punishment," nor requires due process beyond traditional common law remedies. The author argues that this decision reflects the majority's conservative cultural values, which stress the importance of historic tradition, specifically, of Puritan, authoritarian tradition. An analysis of parent-child, teacher-student relationships indicates the tension between democratic and authoritarian concepts in American society.

24. **Student Disciplines: An Analysis of Teacher and Administrator Perceptions.** Camp, William G.; Bourn, Lawton P., Jr. Jun 1979, 31p; Paper presented at the International Congress on Education (2nd, Vancouver, British Columbia, June 17–20, 1979); Table may be marginally legible due to small print (ED 173 971; Reprint: EDRS).

This paper discusses research findings concerning student discipline problems in Indiana secondary schools. Issues explored attempted to determine (1) what specific student behaviors are perceived by teachers and administrators to be discipline problems, (2) how frequently these problems occur, (3) how serious teachers and administrators perceive the problems to be, and (4) how much the identified discipline problems interfere with the learning environment. Questionnaires were mailed to a sample of secondary school teachers and administrators in Indiana. Of the 101 student misbehaviors listed, only 47 were perceived to be discipline problems by a majority of the teachers responding. The paper concludes that teachers who deal with the individual classroom work of the student hold different perceptions of student discipline than administrators who must be concerned with the problems of the school at large. Related literature on the subject of student discipline is reviewed in detail in this document.

25. **A Study of Perceptions of Discipline Problems in Secondary Schools in North Carolina.*** Clarke, James Alexander, The University of North Carolina at Chapel Hill, 1976, 142p (77–17, 310; Reprint: DC).

The purpose of this study was to determine the opinions of students, teachers, and principals relative to selected variables that are concerned with discipline in the public secondary schools of North Carolina. Data on ten basic discipline areas were collected from 1,648 respondents and analyzed by type of respondent, sex, and race of students and faculties, and by the three geographic regions in the state.

In the opinion of the respondents, discipline is a problem of concern in the high schools, and the problem had increased somewhat during the last three years. Principals and teachers reported that the causes of discipline problems were related to societal and home conditions; whereas, students believed the problem was attributed to school conditions and interaction between students and faculties.

The participants in the study reported that a disproportionate number of low academic students were involved in discipline problems; while no particular type, rather than specific sex-race categories, created problems.

With the exception of the destruction of property, the participants thought that most of the behaviors that caused discipline problems at the high school level are minor offenses. According to the survey results, a number of corrective practices are used to reduce discipline problems. Teachers and principals reported that a number of the corrective practices are effective; their students generally disagree. All three types of respondents believed, however, that expulsions and suspensions were justified for the more serious offenses.

In responding to a question concerning the administration of punishment on an equitable basis, a majority of the teachers and principals reported that all students are either treated the same or punishment is administered upon an evaluation of individual needs. In contrast, students reported that favoritism was shown to students who performed high academically and to athletes or other students with special talents.

26. **Violence and Vandalism in the Schools: The Problem and How to Address It.** Deaver, Philip, Ball State University, Muncie, IN, Institute for Community Education Development; National Community Education Association, Flint, MI; Virginia University, Charlottesville, Mid-Atlantic Center for Community Education, 1976, 64p (ED 145 529; Reprint: EDRS–HC not available; also available from Offices of the National Community Education Association, 1017 Avon Street, Flint, MI 48503).

This paper was prepared by members of the National Community Education Association's Committee on Violence and Vandalism in the Schools as a review of the literally hundreds of pounds of information, research, and news generated on this topic. The purpose of this review is to indicate how community education coordinators and directors can constructively approach these problems. The author outlines the scope, causes, and suggested solutions to the complex problems of vandalism and crime, drawing on the report of the Senate Judiciary Subcommittee to Investigate Juvenile Delinquency and other sources. He mentions the difficulty in ascertaining whether the causes for youth crime and violence lies within the schools or within society as a whole. He also briefly summarizes the school security measures taken by some districts, outlines possible long-range process measures to cope with these problems, and delineates community education's potential as a means of solving these problems. Statistics on school vandalism and violence are included.

27. **Violence in the Schools.** Jaslow, Carol K., ERIC Clearinghouse on Counseling and Personnel Services, Ann Arbor, MI, 1978, 53p. Sponsoring agency: National Institute of Education (DHEW), Washington, DC (ED 165 084; Reprint: EDRS; also available from ERIC/CAPS, 2108 School of Education, The University of Michigan, Ann Arbor, MI 48109).

This collection of ERIC documents is designed to identify useful resources for anyone working with problems of violence or vandalism in an educational setting. These documents represent a computer search of the ERIC database covering the period of November, 1966 through May, 1978. The materials reviewed here address the following areas of concern: issues and trends in school violence; methods for coping with violence such as student cooperation, special projects, public relations, and parent education; the Safe Schools Act; and the role of the counselor. Additionally, descriptions of exemplary programs and services specifically designed to deal with school violence are provided.

28. **Violent Schools—Safe Schools.** The Safe School Study Report to the Congress, Volume I. National Institute of Education (DHEW), Washington, DC, Jan 1978, 357p; some parts are marginally legible due to print size (ED 149 464; Reprint: EDRS; also available from Superintendent of Documents, US Government Printing Office, Washington, DC 20402 (Stock No. 017–080–01830–6); Executive Summary—ED 149 466, 12p).

The Safe School Study was mandated by Congress to determine the frequency, seriousness, and incidence of crime in elementary and secondary schools in all regions of the United States; the cost of material replacement and repair; the means used in attempting to prevent crimes in schools; and means by which more effective crime prevention may be achieved. The study is based on a mail survey of over 4,000 schools and an onsite survey of 642 schools, and case studies of 10 schools. Among the findings are that about eight percent of the nation's schools have a serious problem with crime; over 25 percent of all schools are subject to vandalism in a given month; and the annual cost of school crime is estimated to be around $200 million. Security devices and security personnel are considered effective in reducing crime, although more emphasis on personnel training is needed. In the case studies, the single most important difference between safe schools and violent schools was found to be a strong, dedicated principal who served as a role model for both students and teachers, and who instituted a firm, fair, and consistent system of discipline.

BOOKS

29. **Classroom Management. The 78th Yearbook of the National Society for the Study of Education, Part II.** Duke, Daniel, Ed. Chicago: University of Chicago Press, 1979, 447p.

This volume contains research and review articles designed to promote informed discussion of the important issue of discipline and order in the classroom.

Factors in Misbehavior

JOURNAL ARTICLES

30. **Behavior Problems in Secondary Schools.** Feldhusen, John F. *Journal of Research and Development in Education*. v11, n4, p17–28, Sum 1978.

This article reviews and clarifies the problems of antisocial student behavior in schools, ranging from talking out of turn to violent attacks upon fellow students or teachers. It focuses on the high school and junior high school, and attempts to identify causes while examining programs and procedures for remediating or preventing such behavior.

31. **Classroom Discipline: An Exercise in the Maintenance of Social Reality.** Wegmann, Robert G. *Sociology of Education*. v49, n1, p71-79, Jan 1976.

The author examines many common foci of classroom discipline through tape recordings and observations of 12 high school teachers as they went about the process of maintaining discipline.

32. **Crime and Punishment on Campus: An Inner City Case Study.** Cox, Winston B. *Adolescence*. v13, n50, p339–48, Sum 1978 (EJ 188 257; Reprint: UMI).

This case study of a predominately Black, metropolitan high school gives insight into staff and student attitudes about discipline problems, rules, and the mechanics of punishment.

33. **Debating with Untested Assumptions— The Need to Understand School Discipline.** Lufler, Henry S., Jr. *Education and Urban Society*. v11, n4, p450–64, Aug 1979.

This in-depth study of six Wisconsin secondary schools examined the assumptions and processes of school discipline. Results indicated that there is little agreement about what constitutes a rule infraction and what the punishment should be; decisions are made on an individual basis by teachers and principals, which can lead to a pattern of discrimination against certain classes of students. Frequently, little understanding is evidenced of the full meaning of Supreme Court decisions in this area.

34. **Discipline and the Public Schools: Are We as Educators Part of the Problem?** Robinson, Andrew; Bickel, Frank. *Integrated Education.* v16, n2, p9–11, Mar-Apr 1978.

This discussion demonstrates that in some instances what is actually reported as inappropriate student behavior may emanate from teacher-related biases, idiosyncrasies, insensitivities, and perhaps teacher inadequacies.

35. **Due Process and Conduct in Schools.** Chamelin, Neil; Trunzo, Kae B. *Journal of Research and Development in Education.* v11, n2, p74–83, Win 1978 (EJ 176 990; Reprint: UMI).

Examines the reasons for the rapid intervention of courts into areas primarily an administrative decision-making process and describes those areas in which legal decisions have drastically defined and restricted the permissible scope of administrative activity in schools.

36. **Establishing a Workplace: Teacher Control in the Classroom.** LeCompte, Margaret D. *Education and Urban Society.* v11, n1, p87–106, Nov 1978 (EJ 193 519; Reprint: UMI).

This study of teacher behavior in four classrooms reveals that, in the dimension of management, teachers looked rather alike. Where differences did exist, they seemed to be determined by the individual personality and philosophy of the teacher rather than by institutional constraints which dictated the management core.

37. **The Etiology of Student Misbehavior and the Depersonalization of Blame.** Duke, Daniel Linden. *Review of Educational Research.* v48, n3, p415–37, Sum 1978 (EJ 191 559; Reprint: UMI).

The author contends that research in the social sciences has witnessed a depersonalization of blame for individual misbehavior, and examines the process by which the blame for school discipline problems has been transferred from individual students to external factors. Recommendations are made for future research approaches.

38. **Evaluating School Discipline through Empirical-Research.** Clune, William H. *Education and Urban Society.* v11, n4, p440–49, Aug 1979.

This essay examines the problem of developing a widely acceptable set of standards for evaluating school discipline: proposes and defends a group of related standards concerning basic fairness borrowed from American constitutional law; and concludes with a reminder that the discovery of a problem of basic fairness does not necessarily mean that a ''legalistic'' solution is the proper kind.

39. **Factors in School Vandalism.** Howard, James L. *Journal of Research and Development in Education.* v11, n2, p53–63, Win 1978 (EJ 176 988; Reprint: UMI).

Reports on factors relating to school vandalism based on a review of selected literature that included juvenile delinquency. Research and theoretical writings were included for purposes of comparison and conflicting findings were also discussed, as well as common findings. An attempt was made to relate theoretical work with recent applied research findings.

40. **The Fear of Crime in the School Enterprise and Its Consequences.** Lolli, Michael; Sanitz, Leonard D. *Education and Urban Society.* v8, n4, p401–16, Aug 1976.

This paper argues that, in addition to grade retardation, fear of going to school—a fear shared by most parents—might well be a, if not the, crucial factor in the determination to drop out for appreciable numbers of students.

41. **How the Adults in Your Schools Cause Student Discipline Problems—And What to Do about It.** Duke, Daniel Linden. *American School Board Journal.* v165, n6, p29–30, 46, Jun 1978 (EJ 181 476; Reprint: UMI).

Research discovered six categories of adult behavior that lead to student discipline problems—inconsistent rule enforcement, noncompliance with discipline policies, insensitivity, lack of data, lack of classroom management skills, and inadequate administration of discipline policies.

42. **Intrinsic Rewards in School Crime.** Csikszentmihalyi, Mihaly; Larson, Reed. *Crime and Delinquency.* v24, n3, p322–35, Jul 1978. (EJ 184 607; Reprint: UMI).

Proposes that the state of enjoyment occurs when a person is challenged at a level matched to his level of skills. Disruption of classes, vandalism, and violence in schools are, in part, attempts by adolescents to obtain enjoyment in otherwise lifeless schools.

43. **Lessons to be Learned about Discipline from Alternative High Schools.** Perry, Cheryl L.; Duke, Daniel Linden. *Journal of Research and Development in Education.* v11, n4, p78–91, Sum 1978.

Attempts to determine whether behavior problems were as great a concern in schools-within-a-school as they were perceived to be in regular high schools. Uses student and teacher ratings as criteria for evaluating behavior problems.

44. **Looking at the School as a Rule-Governed Organization.** Duke, Daniel Linden. *Journal of Research and Development in Education.* v11, n4, p116–26, Sum 1978.

This article discusses 11 hypotheses that may explain why respect for the school as a rule-governed organization has slipped to such a low status. It suggests that improvement in student behavior may require basic changes in the ways schools are organized and managed.

45. **Misbehavior in Classroom—Anxiety, a Possible Cause.** Leffingwell, R. J. *Education.* v97, n4, p360–63, Sum 1977.

It is the intent of the article to provide a pragmatic overview of the causes of school-related anxiety and ways in which it can be recognized. Practical solutions that the teacher can utilize in a school setting will be offered. A perusal of the research shows that most of the articles written about performance anxiety and its effect on behavior have been done on the college level. This article attempts to provide information derived from research and practical experience in secondary schools.

46. **A New View of the Dynamics of Discipline.** Kindsvatter, Richard. *Phi Delta Kappan.* v59, n5, p322–25, Jan 1978 (EJ 169 844; Reprint: UMI).

Presents a conceptualization of the basic principles of discipline which includes three components of discipline—behavior expectations, behavior adjustment, and control techniques—and three sources of student misbehavior.

47. **Problem Students.** *USA Today.* v108, n2411, p8, Aug 1979 (EJ 213 641; Reprint: UMI).

Reports on a large-scale study which found that 60 percent of students are labeled as "behavior problems" by their teachers at least once during their elementary school careers. Discusses the questions this raises about teacher judgments, school behavior standards, and the impact on student self-concept.

48. **Procedural Due Process in Secondary School Discipline.** Manley-Casimir, Michael E. *Theory into Practice.* v17, n4, p314–20, Oct 1978 (EJ 198 794; Reprint: UMI).

This article uses the Supreme Court decision in Goss v Lopez as a starting point and frame reference for describing and assessing the discipline procedure in one public high school.

49. **Reflections on Classroom Authority.** Tinto, Vincent. *Education and Urban Society.* v11, n1, p107–18, Nov 1978 (EJ 193 520; Reprint: UMI).

Teacher preference may well be the underlying element that determines the association between instructional formats and control activities.

50. **Review Essays.** Milofsky, Carl. *School Review.* v87, n1, p64–71, Nov 1978 (EJ 192 905; Reprint: UMI).

Critically reviews four recent books which focus on disruptive teenagers in schools. General orientation of the books is micro- rather than macro-sociological. Reviewer suggests that some conflict in schools is unavoidable and that pervasive, severe school disruption is an index of fundamental social change.

51. **Teacher Pupil-Control Ideology and Behavior and Classroom Environmental Robustness.** Multhauf, Arleen P. et al. *Elementary School Journal.* v79, n1, p40–46, Sep 1978.

Examines teacher's beliefs and behavior regarding pupil control and their impact on fourth, fifth, and sixth grade students' perceptions of classroom life. Research indicates that humanistic teacher pupil-control behavior is associated with students' reports of high classroom robustness. Inconsistencies between male ideology and behavior are discussed.

52. **Teacher Styles of Classroom Management.** Smith, Douglas K. *Journal of Educational Research.* v71, n5, p277–82, May-Jun 1978 (EJ 197 864; Reprint: UMI).

This study attempts to demonstrate that classroom management style varies among groups of teachers and is influenced by the variables of student behavior and sex of student. For example, teachers use punishment for undesirable behavior more frequently in response to male students than female students.

53. **Teacher Transitions Can Disrupt Time Flow in Classrooms.** Arlin, Marshall. *American Educational Research Journal.* v16, n1, p42–56, Win 1979 (EJ 205 647; Reprint: UMI).

Disruptive pupil behavior increased during teacher-initiated transition time as opposed to nontransitional time. Procedures for structuring transitions to increase time-on-task and maintain smoothness and momentum are described, and teachers' conceptions of time and classroom time flow are discussed.

54. Teachers and Classroom Discipline. Unruh, Adolph. *NASSP Bulletin.* v61, n406, p84–87, Feb 1977.

Discusses eight categories of teacher weaknesses that contribute to classroom discipline problems. They include methods of teaching, general attitudes, rapport with students, and teacher inflexibility.

55. Teachers' Perceptions of and Reactions to Misbehavior in Traditional and Open Classrooms. Solomon, Daniel; Kendall, Arthur J. *Journal of Educational Psychology.* v67, n4, p528–30, Aug 1975.

Suggests that open and traditional classroom settings may create different norms and standards which cause teachers to perceive and react differently to objectively similar child behaviors.

56. The Toughest Game in Town. Koff, Robert H. *NASSP Bulletin.* v63, n424, p8–18, Feb 1979 (EJ 196 050; Reprint: UMI).

Changing social values, recent court decisions, inconsistency in thought and action, and consolidation of schools into massive factories are some of the factors that relate to the problem of student discipline. Some solutions are suggested.

57. Types of Behavior Problems that May Be Encountered in the Classroom. Fremont, Theodore S.; Wallbrown, Fred H. *Journal of Education.* v161, n2, p5–24, Spr 1979.

This paper provides an overview of the different patterns of behavior problems that teachers are likely to encounter in the classroom. Different systems for categorizing learning and behavioral problems are considered. Suggestions for informal observation of classroom behavior are included.

58. Violence in Public Schools: HEW's Safe School Study. Rubel, Robert J. *NASSP Bulletin.* v62, n416, p75–83, Mar 1978 (EJ 173 582; Reprint: UMI).

Selected statistics and findings from HEW's Safe School Study are summarized here, revealing that the secondary school principal is a key figure in reducing school crime and violence.

59. Why Don't Girls Misbehave More than Boys in School? Duke, Daniel Linden. *Journal of Youth and Adolescence.* v7, n2, p141–57, Jun 1978.

In reviewing research, the author speculates on six reasons why girls misbehave less than boys, despite the fact that girls have more personal problems during adolescence. The author concludes that a combination of personal charac-

teristics and external pressures inhibit misbehavior in girls. Over 50 bibliographical references are included.

60. Will the Real Cause of Classroom Discipline Problems Please Stand Up? Timmreck, Thomas C. *Journal of School Health.* v48, n8, p491–97, Oct 1978.

This article addresses the possible causes of discipline problems, concluding that, while causes are many and while the student and the classroom are strong contributors to the problem, the teacher is the major cause of classroom difficulties.

REPORTS

61. All I Bring Is a Radio: A Relational Study of Misbehavior in an Inner-City High School.* Payne, Charles Melvin, Jr., Northwestern University, 1976, 205p (77–1327; Reprint: DC).

The dissertation is concerned with the relative utility of two theoretical approaches to the study of inequality. One approach, the attribute approach, assumes that the significant independent variables are the cultural and psychological attributes of have-nots. The other approach, relational theory, takes as its independent variable the relationship between haves and have-nots. The first chapter argues that sociology has traditionally been dominated by attribute theory, a dominance which cannot be justified on empirical grounds. The aim of the dissertation is to demonstrate the heuristic potential of relational theory, taking the misbehavior of inner-city high school students as a case in point. Thus, an attempt is made to show that a significant proportion of student misbehavior is the result of teacher behaviors. The data were gathered from observation, interviews with students and archival sources in a Chicago high school.

The most striking characteristic of the school studied was its disorganization, a significant portion of which results from teacher misbehavior, which is here conceptualized as a form of exploitation. Observational data are used to suggest that the degree of teacher misbehavior is determined primarily by the degree to which administrators are willing to make demands on teachers. Interview data are used to suggest that the degree of student misbehavior—which is also treated as a form of exploitation—is primarily determined by the degree to which teachers are demanding. The quality of teaching and the degree to which the teacher behaves in an humiliating fashion are also investigated, but they appear less significant than the level of demands invoked by the teacher. Thus, it appears that a relational explanation of misbehavior in inner-city schools is possible.

The final chapter tries to buttress the argument for a relational perspective by demonstrating that such a perspective, especially centering around the level of demands, provides plausible lines of inquiry for a number of important educational issues. Most importantly, it is argued that both the culture deprivation and teacher expectation models of inner-city education are inadequate insofar as they do not take demands into account. Is is also suggested that the pattern of low demands and relatively favorable interpersonal relationships which seems to prevail in inner-city high schools operates as a cooling-out process. It is argued that American schools of whatever type may be moving in the direction of lower demands.

62. An Analysis of the Relationship of Discipline Practices of Teachers and the School Climate.*
Alcorn, Richard Dean, United States International University, 1976, 145p (77–16,395; Reprint: DC).

The problem of the study was to determine if positive practices regarding discipline are related to a positive school climate.

One objective of the study was to test the following hypotheses: (1) There is a relationship between teachers' self-perceptions of discipline practices and school climate in low-income schools, and (2) there is a relationship between teachers' self-perceptions of discipline practices and school climate in middle-income schools.

In addition to testing the above hypotheses, the additional objectives were: (1) to describe discipline practices utilized by teachers in low-income elementary schools; (2) to describe discipline practices utilized by teachers in middle-income schools; (3) to describe the extent to which the perceptions of teachers regarding discipline practices are the same in low- and middle-income schools; and (4) to describe the frequency of use of discipline practices by sex and experience of the teacher in low- and middle-income schools.

All data were secured from responses to a questionnaire designed to be answered by teachers in low- and middle-income schools. The questionnaire, developed by the researcher, contained 42 items divided into 32 statements on school discipline and ten statements on school climate.

Subject groups consisted of 196 teachers in ten low-income and six middle-income schools.

Differences between the means for the various groups were tested through the use of the Spearman rank-difference correlation of coefficient.

The analysis of the data indicated that teachers in low- and middle-income schools used very similar kinds of discipline practices. Teachers in low-income schools used all forms of discipline practices slightly more often than middle-income schools. The discipline practices identified as most positive and beneficial were in the categories of counseling and contact with the home. Male teachers with four or more years experience utilized positive discipline practices most frequently. An important finding showed that teachers in all groups with four or more years experience used positive discipline practices more frequently than teachers with less than four years experience. There was a strong correlation between teachers' self-perceptions of discipline practices and school climate in low-income schools. There was not a significant relation-

ship between discipline practices and school climate in middle-income schools.

The three main conclusions resulting from this study were: (1) there is a strong relationship between the self-perceptions of teachers in low-income schools regarding the use of positive discipline practices and the school climate; (2) male teachers, in both low- and middle-income schools, use positive discipline practices slightly more frequently than female teachers; and (3) teachers with over four years experience use positive discipline practices slightly more frequently than teachers with less than four years experience.

63. Classroom Culture and the Problem of Control. Eric/CUE Urban Diversity Series, Number 63.
Grannis, Joseph C., Columbia University, New York, ERIC Clearinghouse on the Urban Disadvantaged, May 1979, 45p. Sponsoring agency: National Institute of Education (DHEW), Washington, DC (ED 173 501; Reprint: EDRS).

Although classrooms vary in design and populations, there are certain features that are common to virtually all classrooms. These include the crowding of pupils, the compulsion of school attendance, and the expectation that teachers will foster literacy. The manner in which these features are dealt with in a classroom constitutes the core problem of control in schooling. The most common solution to the problem of control is the standard classroom. Alternative classroom settings that appear to be associated with differences among children can best be understood as variations on the standard classroom. In some of these alternatives, higher support conditions and the positive cast of classroom activities seem to reduce the disorder and alienation found in classrooms, particularly with regard to disadvantaged and ethnic minority children. However, as a number of studies suggest, differences stemming from the students' and teachers' styles within a classroom are more prominent than differences between standard and alternative educational settings. These findings indicate that the most significant changes in classrooms would only be possible if the basic conditions of schooling were so altered that the standard classroom simply would not work.

64. Discipline Practices of Secondary School Administrators in Relation to Their Attitudes Regarding Rights of Students.*
Edd, Leon, The University of Oklahoma, 1977, 148p (78–15,356; Reprint: DC).

The investigation was centered around the problem of determining if there were relationships between the discipline practices of secondary public school administrators and their attitudes toward civil and human rights of students. Discipline practices used when dealing with general school policy violations, which would not involve the permanent expulsion of the offending student, were of particular interest in this study.

Eight hypotheses, concerned with the severity of discipline measures (dependent variable) used by secondary school administrators, were posed for testing. Factors of student's gender, race, and offense, were related independent variables in the study. A sample size of 33 secondary school administrators was used from a total population of 67 in suburban and semi-rural Oklahoma County. Each administrator recorded factors of gender, race, offense, and disciplinary action exerted for each referral over a designated period of time.

Data obtained were de-coded and scored to create a disciplinary action score for each administrator. The disciplinary action score was compared to a second score earned by the secondary school administrators, which represented their attitudes regarding civil and human rights of students as measured by The Rights of Students Inventory (David Guilliams, 1972). A Pearson Product Moment Correlation Coefficient, Multiple Analysis of Variance, and Kirk Test of Simple Main Effects were employed in the statistical procedures.

Data analysis indicated that secondary school administrators were not consistent in matching punishment to the severity of the offense. It was indicated that race and gender were significant determining factors in the severity of punishment exerted by secondary school administrators.

65. Misbehavior in High Schools: Its Relationship to Depersonalization, Grade Size, Student-Professional Staff Ratio, and Organizational Pattern.* Peterson, Terrance Kent, University of South Carolina, 1978, 135p (79–11,851; Reprint: DC).

The purpose of this study was to investigate an ecological model of misbehavior which was based on the belief that high schools having a large number of students in each grade, large student-professional staff ratios, composed primarily of young adolescents and possessing many grades, would foster feelings of depersonalization among students in the schools, and, in turn, would encourage student misbehavior.

Three general questions were investigated: (1) Is depersonalization related to misbehavior? (2) Are grade size, student-professional staff ratio and organizational pattern related to depersonalization? (3) Are grade size, student-professional staff ratio, and organizational pattern related to misbehavior?

In answering the first two general questions, the sample consisted of 56 high schools in South Carolina. The variable depersonalization was investigated using eleventh grade students in the schools. In answering the third question, the sample consisted of 206 of the 217 high schools in South Carolina.

A six item self-report was used as a measure of students' feelings of depersonalization in the schools. From data on the student discipline section of the "Individual School Campus Reports," required by the Office for Civil Rights, two indicators of misbehavior were constructed. Grade size referred to the average number of students enrolled in each grade. Student-professional staff ratio referred to the number of students enrolled divided by the number of professional personnel in the schools. Organizational pattern referred to the type of grade combination in the schools (7–12 or 8–12, 9–12, and 10–12 or 11–12).

The most parsimonious ecological model supported by the findings in the investigation is shown below.

Grade Size $\longrightarrow$ Depersonalization $\longrightarrow$ Misbehavior

Only a weak direct relationship existed between grade size and misbehavior and between student-professional staff ratio and misbehavior. Organizational pattern did not appear to be related to depersonalization or misbehavior.

The implications for educational practice were: (1) Administrative and school board actions that result in increasing the number of students in a grade or school (e.g., consolidation of schools, addition of rooms to existing schools, reorganization of schools) should be avoided until the ramifications of such moves on depersonalization, misbehavior, and student participation in activities are carefully considered. (2) Schools that already have large grade and school sizes should find ways to decrease students' feelings of depersonalization and misbehavior through ecological and nonecological changes (e.g., increasing parent involvement, increasing the utilization of various interaction techniques by the faculty, using crisis counseling, employing community education).

66. Order and Disruption in a Desegregated High School. Noblit, George W.; Collins, Thomas W., National Council on Crime and Delinquency, Hackensack, NJ, NewGate Resource Center, Feb 1978, 37p; Chapter 25 of "Theoretical Perspectives on School Crime, Volume I." Sponsoring agency: Department of Health, Education, and Welfare, Washington, DC (ED 157 193; Reprint: EDRS).

One of 52 theoretical papers on school crime and its relation to poverty, this chapter, by utilizing ethnographic data, develops an understanding of the interrelationships among administrative styles, deterrence, commitment, and disruption. The effect of change in administrative styles on the character of order and disruption in a desegregated southern high school is examined. The concern of this paper is primarily with control systems and their effects, and not with the incidence of misbehavior. The data were drawn from an ongoing ethnographic study geared to investigate the process of interracial schooling. Additional data are presented from an ethnography of another high school in a different southern city to facilitate the formulation of conclusions. The paper concludes that a highly representative governance system fosters commitment in the vast majority of school participants. The participants have a major role in making and revising the rules, and thus, when caught violating them, they are hard pressed to question the legitimacy of those rules.

67. Poverty, School Control Patterns, and Student Disruption. Lesser, Philip, National Council on Crime and Delinquency, Hackensack, NJ, NewGate Resource Center, Feb 1978, 52p; Chapter 20 of "Theoretical Perspectives on School Crime, Volume I." Sponsoring agency: Department of Health, Education and Welfare, Washington, DC (ED 157 188; Reprint: EDRS).

One of 52 theoretical papers on school crime and its relation to poverty, this chapter, by exploring the relationships among poverty, the ways schools are organized, and student disruption, generates notions that will help in developing a theoretical perspective on school disruption in terms of the various control patterns of school organization. This analysis suggests that school organizations emphasizing rule-oriented patterns of control experience more disruption than do schools that stress development of student commitment by way of normative controls. The paper begins by examining several research traditions regarding school disruption and reviewing categories of explanations. After discussing the presumed relationship of poverty and school disruption, a theoretical framework based on an organizational analysis of school control is suggested. Finally, solutions to school disruption are discussed in terms of the extent to which they stress either rule-oriented or norm-oriented patterns of control.

68. School Crime and Disruption: Prevention Models. Responsible Action, Inc., Davis, CA. Sponsoring agency: National Institute of Education (DHEW), Washington, DC, Jun 1978, 197p (ED 160 710; Reprint: EDRS; also available from Superintendent of Documents, US Government Printing Office, Washington, DC 20402).

The focus in this anthology is on practical approaches to school crime prevention and control. The collection begins with two papers describing approaches to the study of crime in schools. One of these outlines a strategy for basing prevention programs on the findings of research tailored to a particular school, while the other offers a conceptual framework for studying school crime and taking appropriate actions to prevent it. These papers are followed by a group of articles which are primarily explanatory, suggesting current theories of causation, but which also offer concrete suggestions for altering conditions in school or society which contribute to school crime. Some of the areas discussed in this section include negative school experiences and low self-esteem, aesthetics of vandalism, the lack of meaningful roles for youth in contemporary society, labeling, and the structural and control theories of delinquency. The third category of papers differs from the second primarily in emphasis. While drawing on various theories of crime causation, these papers concentrate on specific programs or actions which can be taken to reduce school crime. Topics dealt with in this section include racial discrimination, student alienation, selection of school board members, school size, training of specialists, cross-age child care, community involvement, and moral education.

69. School Violence and the Social Organization of High Schools. Ianni, Francis A. J., National Council on Crime and Delinquency, Hackensack, NJ, NewGate Resource Center, Feb 1978, 39p; Chapter 15 of "Theoretical Perspectives on School Crime, Volume I." Sponsoring agency: Department of Health, Education, and Welfare, Washington, DC (ED 157 183; Reprint: EDRS).

One of 52 theoretical papers on school crime and its relation to poverty, this chapter, based on the findings of an in-depth study of the social organization of the American high school, provides a new, school-specific way of examining the problem of school crime and violence. The study, which made use of field methodology, addressed two basic questions: "What is the code of rules which makes the high school a social system?" and "How do people learn to play this game?" Data collected enabled researchers to describe four major structural domains of socialization transactions (the teaching-learning structure, the authority-power structure, the peer-group structure, the cross-group structures) and three major processes of social action by which the four structures are operationalized in the social organization (sorting, territoriality, rule making, and rule breaking). It is suggested that this model of the social organization of the American high school, in isolating what is school-specific about crime and violence in schools, may enable educators to develop a means of effectively dealing with the problem.

70. The Social Patterning of Deviant Behaviors in School. Tinto, Vincent et al., National Council on Crime and Delinquency, Hackensack, NJ, New-Gate Resource Center, Feb 1978, 55p; Chapter 37 of "Theoretical Perspectives on School Crime, Volume I." Sponsoring agency: Department of Health, Education, and Welfare, Washington, DC (ED 158 367; Reprint: EDRS).

One of 52 theoretical papers on school crime and its relation to poverty, this chapter attempts to demonstrate that deviant behaviors in school are caused and patterned by the manner in which schools differentially constrain the ability of students legitimately to attain the goal of academic success. By applying a modified and extended version of Merton's model of deviance to an assessment of the available research on student deviancy, the authors show that the occurrence of deviance among students, in both overall rates and types of deviant responses made, is socially patterned within the social system of the school, reflecting the socioeconomic status, racial, and sexual attributes of the student body.

71. A Study of Relationships between Senior High School Enrollment and the Number of Discipline Problems Experienced by Senior High School Administrative Personnel.* Hinson, Gregory Lantz, The University of Akron, 1978, 231p (79–02,975; Reprint: DC).

The purpose of this study was to ascertain whether or not movement towards larger schools in fact results in deleterious effects in terms of school discipline. The study provides background, based on empirically analyzed data, on the relationship between high school size and the number of discipline problems experienced in that school.

The study used an ex post facto research design. This research design was guided by the literature related to the current state of discipline in our nation's schools, literature on discipline per se, literature on school size, and research on the relationship between school size and discipline.

Similarities and differences in the number of discipline problems experienced between small and large high schools were determined by statistical treatment of the data. Multiple linear regression analysis was used to determine F-ratios and probability levels.

When the size of the school is considered alone, two variables proved to be significant: (1) the proportion of assaults on teachers in small and large high schools; and (2) the difference between the proportion of administrator time spent on discipline related topics in small and large high schools. In both cases, however, one must consider the reality of any school setting and include certain variables which impinge upon any school environment. In this study, when the socio-economic status of the students, location of the high school, and minority make-up of the student body are considered in conjunction with the size of the high school, there is no significant difference. Size alone cannot explain a major portion of teacher assaults and amount of administrator time spent on discipline in senior high schools.

An analysis of the means for large and small high schools indicated that large high schools experienced more problems and used a higher proportion of punishments except in the area of detentions and corporal punishments. Small schools tend to employ these sanctions more often than do large high schools.

72. Teacher Control and School Size. Campbell, Lloyd P.; Williamson, John A., 1976, 8p (ED 120 108; Reprint: EDRS).

This study examined the extent to which the size of school enrollment affects teacher control over discipline. The study was limited to high schools in Texas. Fifty high schools were randomly selected from each of five size classifications. A random sample of 750 Texas public high school teachers were selected for the study (150 from each category). Each of the 750 teachers was mailed a 41-item Linkert-type survey instrument which was designed to reveal the degree to which they felt a loss of control over matters of student discipline. Responses were returned from 386 teachers. The study revealed that the size of school enrollment does not affect the teacher's perceived control over matters of student discipline; that is, there were no statistically significant differences among those teachers from each of the five high school classification categories. Analysis of the data further revealed no significant differences when considering the specific variables of teacher age, sex, teaching experience, and subject taught. (The survey instrument is included.)

73. Truancy: An Examination of Social Structual Influences and Traditional Approaches.* Baur, Marilyn S., University of Colorado at Boulder, 1976, 178p (77–3165; Reprint: DC).

The objectives of the research were to test the basic assumptions underlying many school and community policies for dealing with truancy, namely that truants are social isolates, youngsters from unhappy homes, or poor students; to identify other variables related to truancy; to investigate the effects of school social structure upon truancy; and to study the effect upon students of an out-of-school subculture.

A survey questionnaire was completed by 941 junior high school students in three schools. The schools were ranked according to the extent to which their social structures were facilitative of truancy. The policies and practices according to which schools were ranked were identified by interviews with school personnel and community youth workers. Criteria for ranking schools included procedures for taking attendance; penalties for truancy, and policies defining conditions under which students may leave campus.

The school having the social structure most facilitative of truancy had significantly higher rates of self-reported truancy than the other schools (p<.0001). Relatively open attendance policies are believed by some educators to result in students' liking school better. However, proportionately fewer students at the school having the most open policies liked school than did students at the other schools. In addition, students in the more open school were more likely than those in the other schools to believe that teachers did not care about students nor care whether students attend.

Traditional assumptions about causes of truancy were in general not supported by the data. Truancy was not found to be significantly related to social isolation. Unhappy homes were found to be related to truancy only for students whose parents had been officially notified, suggesting that the causal order involving truancy and happiness of home is the opposite of that usually assumed.

Grade point average was found to be significantly related to frequency of truancy. More students who received poor grades were truant than was the case among good students. However, it was not possible in this cross-sectional survey to determine whether poor grades were the cause or the result of the truancy. Perhaps students' grades fall after they begin to skip school.

Shared beliefs of truants were examined, and an explanation was suggested for the weakening of commitment to school which leads to truancy: it is the result of rejected claims to adult status among students who subsequently become truants.

74. Vandalism and School Attitudes.* Murillo, Robert B., The Florida State University, 1977, 403p (77–24,785; Reprint; DC).

Despite the magnitude of the vandalism problem at the present time, relatively little empirical information is available to promote its understanding. This study is an attempt to obtain base level data on several aspects of vandalism which will guide and promote subsequent study into this phenomenon.

This study attempts to accomplish several missions: (1) to test the hypothesis that school vandalism varies with students' school attitudes; (2) to examine the effect of administrative style on the students' school vandalistic behavior; and (3) to conduct a generalized survey of vandalism which is to provide primitive information on the nature and extent of student involvement in vandalism in general, the social academic and demographic correlates of vandalism, and the conditions and factors attending their acts of vandalism.

Because the information sought in this study is normally not available through police records, self-report methodology was employed to acquire information on the subjects' vandalistic and delinquent activity. The extent of the students' vandalistic behavior was measured through their responses on three vandalism checklists especially devised for this study. Other information about the students, their conditions, activities and involvements in the home, school and community was acquired through questionnaires that were administered to three groups of students in three different schools.

Attitudinal information was derived from a generalized attitude scale designed to cover the following subscale dimensions: attitude toward education, perception of teachers, academic self-concept, perception of school relevancy, perception of student powerlessness, perception of relations between teachers and school officials and perception of school administration. Information obtained from these subscales enabled the assessment of student attitudes toward school and administrative style. Additional information on administrative style in the three study schools was obtained in prestudy interviews with school officials.

The findings in this study are that major differences do not appear among the study populations in the three schools with regard to their involvement in vandalism, their attitudes toward school or even their perceptions-evaluations of administrative style. It was found that generally the more alienated the student, as measured by the generalized attitude scale and other questionnaire items, the greater the involvement in vandalism in general and school vandalism in particular.

The underlying theoretical perspective of this study is that of control theory, and the findings, in the main, tend to validate control theory as a suitable vehicle to the analysis of attitudes and vandalism.

Among other findings, vandalism as an activity usually involves little planning, is seldom done alone or in retaliation, and damage behavior is usually highly diversified.

Finally, it is quite apparent that much additional research is needed to replicate aspects of this and other studies and to explore and develop insights and notions about this phenomenon as suggested by vandalism research to date.

BOOKS

75. Classrooms and Corridors: The Crisis of Authority in Desegregated Secondary Schools. Metz, Mary Haywood. Berkeley, CA: University of California Press, 1978, 285p.

Sociological perspectives are employed in this study of two desegregated junior high schools with racially and socioeconomically similar student bodies. The different ways staff members, students, and administrators in the two schools address the tasks of pursuing education while maintaining safety and order are analyzed. Situations and incidents indicative of authority and control are described in terms of social structures and processes which shape behavior, actions of formal and informal leaders, and tension, conflict, and crisis. Contradictions between the bureaucratic structures and the teachers' need for autonomy in dealing with technological problems are used to illustrate organizational impact on social structures. The sources of data are described and a comprehensive bibliography is also included.

Discipline Programs and Practices: Descriptions and Evaluations

Existing Practices and General Methods Research

JOURNAL ARTICLES

76. Contrasting Solutions for School Violence. I. The Crackdown. Wint, Joseph. *Phi Delta Kappan.* v57, n3, p175–76, Nov 1975.

Mr. Wint describes his approach to school violence—the crackdown approach. He believes that strong principals who set a tone of vigilance in the school are necessary to curb violence.

77. Contrasting Solutions for School Violence. II. The Humanitarian Approach. Van Avery, Dennis. *Phi Delta Kappan.* v57, n3, p177–78, Nov 1975.

Mr. Van Avery subscribes to the humanitarian approach to school discipline, fearing that the "law and order" approach is self-defeating in the long run.

78. A Faculty Trains Itself to Improve Student Discipline. Grantham, Marvin L.; Harris, Clifton S., Jr. *Phi Delta Kappan.* v57, n10, p661–64, Jun 1976.

The best approach to discipline is a preventive one—the provision of a variety of educational and environmental alternatives that will interest, challenge, and motivate the pupil. This study at Marcus School, Dallas, Texas, supports the findings of Jacob Kounin that the correlation between teachers' styles of dealing with issues and pupil behavior are higher and more consequential than sometimes thought.

79. Violence in the Schools: Everybody Has Solutions. *American School Board Journal.* v162, n1, p27–37, Jan 1975.

Reports results of a mail survey on the best solutions to crime and violence in schools and presents a variety of proposals by individuals concerned with the problem.

REPORTS

80. An Analysis of the Relationship between Student Codes of Conduct and Student Behavior.* Turner, Andrew J., The University of Michigan, 1978, 223p (78-23,025; Reprint: DC).

Ten public high schools in Wayne County, Michigan were randomly selected to participate in this study.

The participants included all members of the following departments at the selected schools: (1) language, (2) social studies, (3) vocational, and (4) mathematics and science. All participants were given the self-administered questionnaire at faculty meetings by a school official. The participants returned 61.2 percent of the distributed questionnaires.

The statistical analyses of the data used included: (1) mean scores, (2) percentages, (3) Pearson correlation coefficient, and (4) Chi-Square test. Other results were presented in tables and graphs. Scatter plots were used to illustrate relationships between variables.

A number of relevant findings were revealed by the study data. There was general agreement among the teachers concerning the low level of influence student codes of conduct were having on student behavior at their schools. The mean score rankings consistently indicated that student codes of conduct were having very little impact on specific types of student behaviors. Behaviors such as tardiness and smoking on school property were regularly ranked ahead of other behaviors as the most observed student conduct. The data revealed that the codes of student conduct appeared to be somewhat more effective in regulating the most serious types of student behaviors.

A majority of the teachers perceived student codes as having little or no influence on student behaviors affecting the learning atmosphere in the classroom. However, the teachers tended to perceive student codes of conduct as having greater influence on high school seniors than on high school sophomores. Only the social studies teachers differed with fellow teachers on that question.

The Chi-square scores indicated some disagreement among the participants based on demographic variables. For some behaviors, sex, years of teaching experience, and departmental affiliations were significant factors in the participants' responses to specific student behaviors.

81. Classroom Discipline. Research Action Brief Number 5. Oregon University, Eugene, ERIC Clearinghouse on Educational Management, Aug 1979, 5p. Sponsoring agency: National Institute of Education (DHEW), Washington, DC (ED 173 898; Reprint: EDRS; also available from ERIC Clearinghouse on Educational Management, University of Oregon, Eugene, OR 97403).

This research action brief describes five studies designed to test techniques for decreasing disruptive student conduct in the secondary school classroom. The two behavior modification studies discussed showed strong positive results. Questions remain, however, concerning the permanence of behavior changes that are dependent on reward systems and concerning the wisdom of associating appropriate behavior with rewards not intrinsic to the behavior itself. The two humanistic studies in class management concentrated on the rapport created between students and teachers. The first involved teaching communication techniques to teachers, while the second revealed that alternative schools suffer from far fewer disciplinary problems than do traditional schools. The fifth study combined elements of both types of approach. A high level of interaction between teacher and student, derived from humanist thinking, was used as the reward in a system derived from behavior modification.

82. Classroom Management in the Elementary Grades. Research Series No. 32. Brophy, Jere L.; Putnam, Joyce G., Michigan State University, East Lansing, Institute for Research on Teaching, Oct 1978, 131p. Sponsoring agency: National Institute of Education (DHEW), Washington, DC (ED 167 537; Reprint: EDRS; also available from Institute for Research on Teaching, 252 Erickson Hall, East Lansing, MI 48824).

The literature on elementary school management is reviewed. Topics include student characteristics and individual differences, preparing the classroom as a learning environment, organizing instruction and support activities to maximize student engagement in productive tasks, developing workable housekeeping procedures and conduct rules, managing groups during instruction, motivating and shaping desired behavior, resolving conflict and dealing with students' personal adjustment problems, and orchestration of these elements into an internally consistent and effective system. Promising teacher education approaches are discussed in the closing section.

83. Classroom Organization at the Beginning of School: Two Case Studies. Anderson, Linda M.; Evertson, Carolyn M., Texas University, Austin, Research and Development Center for Teacher Education, Jun 1978, 52p; Paper presented at the Annual Meeting of the American Association of Colleges for Teacher Education (30th, Chicago, IL, February 21-24, 1978). Sponsoring agency: National Institute of Education (DHEW), Washington, DC (ED 166 193; Reprint: EDRS).

Observation of two third-grade teachers during the opening days of school revealed different approaches to organizing their classes and instructing pupils on correct classroom behavior. The results of observation are given in narrative form and analyzed. Five principles that characterized the most effective teacher are presented: (1) The teacher who was better organized demonstrated an ability to analyze the tasks of the first weeks of school and presented them to students in small easily understood steps; (2) Before the morning began, the better-organized teacher had clear expectations about what she would accept in the students' behavior and what would be encouraged; (3) The better-organized teacher communicated her expectations clearly to the students from the beginning; (4) The better-organized teacher remained sensitive to the students' concerns and needs for information; and (5) The better-organized teacher monitored her students closely in order to give immediate feedback. Follow-up questions from the classroom organization study are appended.

84. A Critical Examination of Disciplinary Theories and Practice. Sussman, Susan, York Borough Board of Education, Toronto (Ontario), Jun 1976, 120p; not available in hard copy due to marginal legibility of original document (ED 128 955; Reprint: EDRS; also available from The Board of Education for the Borough of York, 2 Trethewey Drive, Toronto, Ontario M6M 4A8).

This report focuses on what is known about the development and control of human behavior that is relevant to school teachers. It examines and summarizes several approaches to behavior management—behavior modification, group dynamics, Glasser's reality therapy approach, the Adlerian approach espoused by Dreikurs, Kohlberg's theory of moral development, and learning theory. The actual and ideal involvement of students and teachers in decision making is explored and the relationship between teachers' attributes and classroom management is discussed. The report is based on published materials and is relevant at the elementary and secondary levels. It is supplemented by a report on a survey of local elementary school teachers' opinions of and attitudes toward classroom management and related issues.

85. A Descriptive Analysis of Pupils' Perceptions of the Use of Reward and Punishment.* Richburg, Jeff Edward, Michigan State University, 1976, 134p (77–5874; Reprint: DC).

The purpose of this study was to analyze the effect of certain reward and punishment techniques used by elementary school teachers when applied according to the moral development stage of the pupil with whom they are used. In addition, an attempt was made to determine whether it is possible to derive from the Kohlberg model a more useful procedure for analyzing descriptions of a teacher's approach to rewards and punishments, and whether there is a reasonable basis for assuming that teachers who have a well-conceived rationale for selecting a certain reward and/or punishment for their individual pupils have more success in social control in the classroom. It was felt to be especially important that educators fully understand the concepts that underlie the use of reward and punishment and why particular rewards and punishments are effective with certain, but not all, pupils.

Data were collected from all teachers in grades 3, 4, and 5 at a single school in which 99 percent of the pupils were White, middle class, and whose parents were predominantly college educated. There were two teachers at each of the three grade levels mentioned—three females and three males.

The teachers involved in the study were asked to provide the names of four students with whom they felt they had in the past been successful in using a reward or punishment to get the student to comply with the teacher's standard of acceptable behavior. The teachers were asked to describe, in a general way, the kinds of rewards and punishments they used, which ones were effective or ineffective, and what they thought were reasons for their effectiveness or ineffectiveness. Each teacher was also asked to name four different students with whom he or she had been unsuccessful. Additionally, each teacher related an episode that involved each of the eight pupils. The teacher described each student's behavior in the episode and told how s/he attempted to get the student to comply with his/her standard of classroom behavior. Two judges decided whether the teacher's approach in attempting to get the pupil to comply would appeal to a child at stage 1, 2, 3, 4, 5, or 6 of the Kohlberg model of moral development, which was selected for use in analyzing the teachers' responses.

It was concluded on the basis of the findings that teachers who adapted their rewards and punishments to fit the individual characteristics of their students were perceived by their students as more effective in control of social behavior in the classroom.

It was also concluded that teachers who had a well-conceived rationale had more success in social control in the classroom when success was defined as pupil satisfaction with the management strategy used by their teacher. In addition, the Kohlberg model was found to be useful in providing a description of a teacher's pupil management strategies.

86. Discipline Practices in the Hillsborough County Public Schools. Foster, Gordon, Miami University, Coral Gables, FL, South Florida School Desegregation Consulting Center, Apr 1977, 82p; best copy available. Sponsoring agency: Office of Education (DHEW), Washington, DC (ED 145 575; Reprint: EDRS-HC not available).

This study consists of an analysis of suspension patterns; a description of inhouse suspension programs; perceptions of secondary principals, teachers, and students about discipline in the schools; perceptions of the community about suspension and discipline policies; a review of the district's human relations program; an examination of student handbooks; and general recommendations and possible alternatives to current practices. Among the conclusions and recommendations are that a significant number of suspensions occur for minor offenses that are nondisruptive, that the suspension rate for Black students is clearly disproportionate to their numbers in the school system, that inhouse suspension programs are perceived as the clearest and quickest way to decrease discipline problems, that suspension should be used sparingly because of its disruption to the individual's education, and that regularly scheduled and planned communication sessions should be maintained and continued between minority group representatives and various levels of the school administration.

87. Discipline Techniques Utilized in Selected Missouri Secondary Schools.* Lea, Dennis Ray, University of Missouri—Columbia, 1978, 166p (79-15,261; Reprint: DC).

It was the purpose of this study to ascertain to what extent various disciplinary techniques were utilized in Missouri secondary classrooms and how they related to selected teacher characteristics including teacher classroom discipline ability.

The following techniques were found to have a significant relationship with the discipline ability rating of the teachers and other selected teacher characteristics used in this study.

1. Teachers and their principals do not generally agree on the rating of classroom discipline ability of teachers.

2. Teachers rated by their principals as superior or excellent teachers in classroom discipline ability use the following discipline techniques less frequently than teachers rated above average, average, or needs improvement:

Talk with principal about the student.
Change the seat of a student who is disruptive.
Isolate the offending student from class.
Lower the student's grade for the day.
Take away privileges of a student or a class.
Call student's parents.
Have a conference with student and principal.
Send pupil to principal's office.
Lower term grade of the student.

3. Teachers rating themselves as superior or excellent teachers in classroom discipline ability use the following discipline techniques less frequently than teachers rated above average, average, or needs improvement.

Send student to counselor's office.
Change the seat of a student who is disruptive.
Isolate the offending student from the class.
Give student a menial task to do.
Have a conference with student and principal.
Send discipline referral slip to the office about student.
Ask that student be transferred to another class.

4. Teachers in the age group of 21–35 years more frequently use the following discipline techniques than the 36–64 age group:

> Direct a question at the inattentive student.
> Give a pop quiz or test to the class.
> Take away privileges of a student or class.
> Give student a menial task to do.

5. Male teachers use the following discipline techniques more frequently than female teachers:

> Criticize the student in front of class.
> Use sarcasm with student or class.

6. Teachers with only bachelor's degrees use the following discipline techniques more frequently than teachers with master's degrees or higher.

> Give a student a special responsibility in class.
> Talk with other teachers about student.
> Give a pop quiz or test to class.
> Lower student's grade for the day.
> Take away privileges of a student or class.
> Ask student to apologize for behavior.
> Send a discipline referral slip to the office about the student.

7. Teachers with 0–5 years in a particular building use the following discipline techniques more frequently than teachers with 6–36 years in a building.

> Talk to the counselor about student.
> Assign extra work to the offending student or class.
> Give a pop quiz or test to the class.
> Take away privileges of a student or a class.
> Give student a menial task to do.

8. Teachers with 0–5 years experience in teaching use the following discipline techniques more frequently than teachers with 6–36 years experience:

> Use a firm tone of voice when dealing with a student or a class problem.
> Assign extra work to the offending student or class.
> Take away privileges of a student or a class.
> Give student a menial task to do.

88. Disruptive Youth: Causes and Solutions. National Association of Secondary School Principals, Reston, VA, 1977, 38p (ED 144 199; Reprint: EDRS-HC not available; also available from National Association of Secondary School Principals, 1904 Association Drive, Reston, VA 22091).

This monograph examines the causes of student disruption and proposes some practical solutions, based on the work of Maryland's 1975 Task Force on Educational Programs for Disruptive Youth. Primary purpose of the Maryland task force was to identify appropriate programs for young people who cannot function in the contemporary school setting. To determine the magnitude and nature of disruptive student behaviors, the task force analyzed questionnaire data supplied by administrators from schools enrolling 75 percent of Maryland's grades 7–12 students. Based on this analysis, the task force recommended five basic types of programs, including (1) a continuum of alternatives and services for students with problems, (2) human relations training for all segments of the school population, (3) expanded counseling services, (4) community diagnostic/treatment centers, and (5) specialized teacher training. Much of the monograph discusses these five programs, including the assumptions upon which each program is based and the rationale for its adoption. The appendix summarizes responses to the task forces' statewide administrator survey.

89. The "Great Man" System of Discipline in Chicago Inner-City High Schools: A Barrier to Educational Goals and Student Rights.* Smith, Richard Clyde, Northwestern University, 1975, 133p (75–29,754; Reprint: DC).

The purpose of this study was twofold: first, to show that the discipline systems operating in Chicago's inner-city high schools violated the discipline philosophy of contemporary educators and sociologists, were ineffective as rehabilitative or preventive institutions, and were open to successful legal challenge; second, to present alternative means of handling discipline problems in the schools that conform to legal restraints imposed upon school officials by recent court decisions affecting the rights of students in the public schools.

Nine characteristics and procedures which describe the "great man" system of discipline are presented, along with an examination of the sections of *Rules: Board of Education of the City of Chicago* which deal with discipline procedures in the public schools. Special note is made of the fact that Chicago has no uniform code of discipline and, therefore, school discipline procedures are determined by individual principals. The problem thus becomes manifest: judicious disciplinary treatment for students is determined by the principal or his agent, the "great man," and too often this vast discretionary power is abused by that agent.

Ten schools were examined in the study. They were located in eight of the ten poorest communities in Chicago. Support for the charges against the "great man" system of discipline was derived from an in-depth examination of the discipline system in one of the schools which was established as representative of the other nine.

The results of the study support the charges against the "great man" discipline system, and three recommendations aimed at amending it are presented: (1) Students should share in the rule-making process. (2) The paragraphs of the *Rules* dealing with suspensions and expulsions should be amended to conform to recent court decisions. (3) The discipline systems in the inner-city high schools should be decentralized.

90. The Identification of Discipline Problems and the Effectiveness of Procedural Controls as Reported by Principals and Physical Education Teachers from Selected Public High Schools in the State of Louisiana, 1975.* Haley, James Rudolph, Northwestern State University of Louisiana, 1976, 250p (77-8684; Reprint: DC).

Questionnaire and personal interviews were administered to principals and physical education teachers of 71 public high schools in Louisiana to identify current discipline problems and procedural control. Schools classified as large, medium, and small were randomly selected from three Public Service Commission Districts.

Major discipline problems were: fighting, class disturbance, smoking, excessive tardiness, disrespect to teachers, unexcused absence, unauthorized leaving of the campus, profanity, stealing, excessive absences, tobacco possession, and truancy. Effective disciplinary procedures were: short-term suspension, long-term suspension, and expulsion. Paddling and spanking, used extensively, were considered ineffective. Significant differences between principals and teachers concerned: use of clinics during school hours, increase of discipline problems, more discipline problems created in nonsport, extra-curricular activities, unawareness of private schools in communities, and the existence of a printed code of conduct.

Data from schools classified by size revealed: small schools favored paddling or spanking; large and medium schools noted football as the sport where most problems occur, while small schools noted baseball; small schools did not favor expulsion and unawareness of existing written codes of conduct.

No significant differences existed in schools classified by Public Service Commission District.

Data not treated statistically revealed: a small percentage of students need to be removed from schools; most problems occur at recess or lunch near rest rooms; most students graduate; most drop-outs are White males; most expulsions are of White males and Black females; few teachers control discipline; and 25 percent of a school day is required for disciplinary problems.

Agreement was revealed between principals and teachers, school sizes, and PSCD's concerning: principals and teachers have become less strict; elective physical education has increased discipline problems; physical education teachers are better disciplinarians; strong physical education and athletic programs deter disciplinary problems and participants create fewer problems; basketball sport creates fewer disciplinary problems; suspensions, expulsions, and compulsory attendance laws are needed; alternative programs are needed; public school disciplinary problems result in children enrolling in private schools; teachers expect principals to control discipline; high achievers create more discipline problems; and confusion exists regarding the existence of printed codes of conduct.

Procedural controls revealed as: very effective—short-term suspension, detention hall after school, school away

from school, writing lines or paragraphs, memory work, lowering grades, and clinic during school hours; as ineffective—long-term suspension, paddling or spanking, detention halls, clinics on weekend or holidays, themes, and standing in hall; and as effective sometimes—punishment jobs at school.

Agreement to interview items revealed:L principals control discipline; undergraduate preparation prepared principals and teachers for disciplinary problems; police are needed on special instances; regular diplomas should not be given to students in alternative programs; and health educators are needed for health related disciplinary problems.

Correlations were related to: common agreement on types of problems and procedural controls; no organizational or administrative pattern for specific disciplinary offenses; expulsion was needed for chronic misbehavers; disiplinary problem increases resulting from teachers and principals becoming less strict; specific control measures are needed for inter-scholastic sports; poor communication between teachers, students, and administrators; recognized need exists for firm school policies to control tardiness; absenteeism, and classroom behavior; organization is needed to decrease problems at lunch rooms and rest rooms; strong athletic and physical education programs are needed to deter discipline problems; health educators are needed; and teachers and principals may be classed as liberals or conservatives regarding the identification, existence, and treatment of disciplinary problems.

91. An Investigation of Discipline Techniques Used by Effective Teachers.* Howard, Rose Ann, George Peabody College for Teachers, 1978, 123p (79-09,955; Reprint: DC).

Educators, and the public in general, view classroom discipline as a perennial school problem. Regardless of societal conditions or any other purported causes which have increased discipline problems, establishing a teaching-learning climate within the schools is predominately a teacher responsibility.

This study examined the discipline techniques of 184 teachers who were selected by their principals as working effectively with their students within the Jefferson County, Kentucky School System. The instrument used was the Survey of Discipline Techniques of Effective Teachers (SDTET) which was developed by the author. It allowed the respondents to match a specific problem with a specific technique and to rate as desirable a list of positive discipline practices. The questionnaire also incorporated the participants' professional experience and educational background. The Pupil Control Ideology (PCI) Form was used to determine participants' beliefs about student discipline.

Descriptive statistics yielded the most and least preferred techniques for each of the 15 problems and the highest rated positive discipline practices. For the ten most popular techniques the Chi-square test of independence was used to compare differences attributed to such variables as: number of years experience, location of population served, and PCI scores.

The findings from this study indicate that there is no clear-cut preference for a single method of discipline. The choice of disicipline techniques appears to be influenced by such things as: seriousness of the problem, teacher beliefs about student control, location of population served, and stated school policies.

Differences were found in this study between discipline techniques favored by the humanistically oriented teachers and those favored by the custodially oriented teachers. Years of teaching experience appeared to be less influential upon the choice of techniques than did the location of population served, urban or suburban. Urban teachers appeared to be less alarmed when confronted with serious problems and chose less stringent discipline approaches for annoying kinds of problems than did their suburban counterparts.

According to this study, neither teacher education programs nor school systems have given priority to the existing discipline problem. Numerous means of utilizing findings of the present study are presented and the need for additional research is discussed.

92. Maintaining Control: Teacher Competence in the Classroom. Eisenhart, Margaret Dec 1977, 19p; Paper presented at the Annual Meeting of the American Anthropological Association (76th, Houston, TX, December 2, 1977) (ED 154 098; Reprint: EDRS).

To be a competent teacher, the school environment must be organized to preserve a system of student behavior and group functioning which allows the teacher to select the activities in which the group will engage. This is often called "maintaining control" by teachers. Means of organizing the school context to affect student behavior are examined in this study. These means include: (1) the arrangement of the physical environment and the people in it; (2) the use of time; and (3) the system of rewards and recognition. The ways in which teachers utilize these means are discussed in terms of their differential success in maintaining control.

93. Procedures for Teachers of the Severely Handicapped to Follow in Controlling Serious Behavior Problems within the Classroom. Change Episode Two. Johnson, James R., La Verne College, CA, 1977, 78p; Doctoral Program in School Management (ED 165 396; Reprint: EDRS).

The report documents a problem-solving approach to the adoption of procedures or dealing with serious behavior problems of severely emotionally disturbed and autistic students in California public schools. Summarized are a review of the literature, an analysis of general techniques of student control, and a list of advantages and disadvantages of such behavior control strategies as physical intervention, time out, and corporal punishment. The end product of the project is explained to be an approved policy list of eight types of

behavior control for use by classroom teachers. Specific procedures are described (including parent involvement), and maximum duration information is listed.

94. Reducing Violence, Vandalism and Disruption in the Schools. A Special Report. New Jersey State Department of Education, Trenton, NJ, May 1979, 287p; Prepared by the Task Force on Reducing Violence and Vandalism; some appendices may be marginally legible (ED 170 949; Reprint: EDRS).

New Jersey's state board of education formed a task force in 1978 to conduct a six-month study of the effectiveness of various strategies for reducing violence and vandalism in the schools. The 47 recommendations developed by the task force were of three types: those designed to improve state-level capabilities (areas addressed included creation within the department of education of an Office to Prevent Crime and Disruption, improved crime reporting, revised requirements for school personnel, improved data collection, the juvenile justice system, and funding possibilities); those to improve local school or school district capabilities (discipline, governance, staff protection, curriculum, school climate, and so forth); and those to improve cooperation between school and community (advisory councils, local planning, community use of schools, and school/police liaison programs). The rationale for these recommendations is presented in this report, and the legal, financial, and time dimensions for carrying out the recommendations are discussed. Extensive appendices include four significant reports on violence and vandalism in New Jersey schools, task force reports on onsite visitations and public hearings, and citation of relevant New Jersey legislation.

95. A Review of Selected Research Findings Pertaining to Classroom Discipline.* Puckett, Ray Boyd, Jr., Saint Louis University, 1978, 258p (79-23,668; Reprint: DC).

The project involved an intensive and extensive search of the periodical literature and ERIC for research and review articles dealing directly and indirectly with aspects of discipline, both inside and outside of the classroom. The essence of the project involved an investigation and presentation of selected research findings and reviews of discipline in an attempt to relate such toward a meaningful discourse that might be employed by teachers in the disposition of their duties.

Exactly 946 individual research studies pertaining to discipline were investigated, categorized, and utilized to support 114 generalized research findings.

The combined 1,060 individual research and review articles dealt with a variety of subjects. Such pertinent items as discipline research, rating devices, attitudes, social pressures, parent and teacher behavior, characteristics of behavioral problem children, environmental influences on behavior, punishment, aggression, school discipline, self control, and behavior modification procedures were included.

The findings of the project were diverse and subject to individual scrutiny. A lengthy and detailed bibliography was provided for follow-up study.

The findings gave support to a number of conclusions. Problems were found to exist in discipline research, rating scales continued to be controversial, and certain children were found to possess and/or exhibit certain traits and are affected by the environment in such a manner as to be identifiable with characteristics generally associated with problem behavior. In addition, evidence was gathered linking aggression to behavior and parents' and teachers' influence on students. Support for specific measures to implement disciplinary, self-control and behavior modification procedures were found to be lacking. Finally, a wide disparity of agreement was found to exist concerning the seriousness of certain behavior problems.

The general concern of all 1,060 articles noted the need for further research.

96. Student Rights and Discipline: Policies, Programs, and Procedures. Moody, Charles D., Ed. et al., Michigan University, Ann Arbor, School of Education, 1978, 193p. Sponsoring agency: Office of Education (DHEW), Washington, DC (ED 160 926; Reprint: EDRS—HC not available; also available from Dr. Charles D. Moody, Sr., Director, Program for Educational Opportunity, 1046 School of Education, The University of Michigan, Ann Arbor, MI 48109).

This compilation of papers from Program for Educational Opportunity conferences incorporates theoretical, empirical, legal, and programmatic perspectives pertinent to the regulation of student behavior in the desegregated setting. The dual challenge of protecting students' rights and teaching socially responsibile behavior is explored. The legal aspects of suspension as a disciplinary technique are explained in terms of impact of Supreme Court rulings. Personal liability of teachers is outlined in cases where constitutional rights are violated. Because of legal involvement and educational reexamination of school disciplinary actions, particularly removal from school, school districts are seeking alternative means of dealing with student misconduct. Many alternatives are discussed: policy analysis, staff development, community involvement, and a number of organizational modifications. The focus of the individual papers is to provide educational practitioners and policy makers with alternative means of promoting social responsibility and to emphasize the need to scrupulously adhere to due process procedures.

97. Successful Strategies for the Treatment of Identified Student Discipline Issues as Perceived by Elementary School Principals.* Williamson, Noah Elmer, University of Southern California, 1979 (03306-50; Reprint: DC).

The purpose of the study was to determine those practices and characteristics utilized by and found in elementary school teachers and principals and recommended by authorities in the field which lead to a decrease in the number of disruptive incidents or discipline problems by students.

Major findings of the study included: (1) Written codes of conduct are common in the schools, principals believe they are useful, and principals believe that teachers provide the most important input into them. (2) Elementary principals believe that the teacher who is able to reduce discipline problems must be consistent, firm, well organized, and one who enjoys teaching. (3) Principals see student behavior problems as increasing due to the increase in (a) breakup of family unit, (b) student disrespect, (c) parent apathy, (d) student apathy, and (e) parent abusiveness. (4) Principals perceive that they have lost authority to deal with disruptive behavior. (5) Principals believe that the actions which would be most helpful in dealing with disruptive students are (a) elimination of tenure, (b) provision of a "time out" room for disruptive students, (c) an "in school suspension" facility, (d) legal use of corporal punishment without prior parent approval, and (e) longer suspensions. (6) School characteristics which foster a reduction in disruptive behavior are seen to be (a) friendly teachers, (b) warm classroom atmosphere, (c) organized playground activities, (d) small class size and (e) small school size.

Data based conclusions included: (1) The classroom teacher is the single most crucial ingredient in a successful formula to prevent/solve student discipline problems in the classroom. (2) The principal is the single most crucial ingredient in a successful formula to solve student disruption problems in the school. (3) Teacher and principal must choose an approach to discipline with which s/he can project an *authentic, consistent,* and *fair* image to those whom s/he would discipline, for these characteristics, plus the teacher's/principal's *attitude* and *expectations* of students, are the most crucial in the student discipline formula.

98. Teacher Responses to Classroom Misbehavior: Influence Methods in a Perilous Equilibrium.* Deflaminis, John Alfred, University of Oregon, 1975, 305p (76-5156; Reprint: DC).

This study had a twofold purpose. The first was to determine which methods of influence were used by teachers to control pupils who exhibited various types of disruptive misbehavior. The second purpose of this study was to determine why teachers chose those specific methods of control.

Influence was considered from the perspective of the person being influenced (the student). Six methods of influence were defined and utilized: authority, coercion, situational and relational contract, persuasion, and manipulation. These six influence methods were grouped into three categories of influence (unwilling, willing, and unwitting) which were used to describe how the teacher's judgment was substituted for the students'.

Eighty-five certified classroom teachers from Eugene, Oregon, comprised the sample for this study. This sample covered grade levels 1-12. While the school district selected the schools in the sample, volunteers were recruited from the faculties to complete the instrument (Influence Inventory). A stratified random sample of 40 teachers was selected from this population to participate in a follow-up interview.

The Influence Inventory contained 16 hypothetical situations to which teachers responded. Each situation contained a combination of four facets:

1. Duration of disruptive misbehavior.
2. Students' motivation to learn
3. Sex of student
4. Student's ability group

A follow-up interview was used in this study to elicit the teacher's subjective reasons for using the methods of influence chosen in the hypothetical situations.

Authority and coercion (unwilling category) were the most frequently employed methods of influence. Authority and persuasion were the best-liked methods. Authority was most often used because of its expeditious and noninterrupting qualities. Coercion and the two contracts were the least-liked methods.

An unexpected finding was that teachers tended to use the methods of influence in sequence—employing the most expedient (authority, coercion, and manipulation) at the time of a misbehavior and following later with persuasion. This occurred, however, only with persistent disruptive misbehavior.

The sex of the teacher made no discernible difference. The amount of teacher education revealed a relationship opposite to that predicted; less educated teachers used less unwilling methods than those teachers with better education. The most unwilling methods were used in the junor high school, and the high school and elementary school followed as predicted. Much between-school variance was found in the methods used by individual schools. Both age of the teacher and total years as a teacher produced a bi-modal relationship, with the lowest and highest years employing the greatest frequency of unwilling methods. The prediction that unwilling methods were used most often in the first years of a teacher's experience was confirmed.

The most important facet in the smallest space analysis was the duration of the misbehavior. The unwilling category contained more temporary disruptive situations than any other category. Motivated, low-ability students tended to receive more willing treatment than their high-ability counterparts when they committed temporary disruptive misbehavior, but more unwilling treatment with persistent disruptive misbehavior. Motivation was the second most important facet. Unwilling methods were used with nonmotivated students in 75 percent of the situations. The least important facet in the teacher's frame of reference was the student's sex.

Corporal Punishment

JOURNAL ARTICLES

99. All in the Name of the 'Last Resort': The Abuse of Children in American Schools. Mauer, Adah. *Inequality in Education.* n23, p21–28, Sep 1978 (EJ 193 522; Reprint: UMI).

Studies have indicated that corporal punishment in the schools increases, rather than eliminates, delinquency. Some brutal measures taken by school officials (particularly principals and athletic coaches) have caused not only retaliatory vandalism by students, but also parental lawsuits.

100. Are Teachers Becoming More Humane? Levine, Mary Ann. *Phi Delta Kappan.* v59, n5, p353–54, Jan 1978 (EJ 169 854; Reprint: UMI).

Exactly 100 of the 360 teachers responding to a questionnaire on disciplinary tactics opposed the use of corporal punishment in all instances of student misbehavior.

101. The Benighted Status of U.S. School Corporal Punishment Practice. Boonin, Tobyann. *Phi Delta Kappan.* v60, n5, p395–96, Jan 1979 (EJ 193 994; Reprint: UMI).

According to a survey of all 50 state commissioners or superintendents of education, 40 states authorize school corporal punishment by law. Only two states (Massachusetts and New Jersey) neither legally authorize nor administer corporal punishment.

102. Corporal Punishment: The Legality of the Issue.
Harris, J. John, III; Fields, Richard E. *NOLPE School Law Journal.* v7, n1, p88–103, 1977 (EJ 173 616; Reprint: UMI).

Briefly outlines state legislation and reviews court decisions involving the corporal punishment of students by school administrators and teachers. Examines the implications of recent court decisions and offers guidelines for school officials.

103. Corporal Punishment after Ingraham: Looking to State Law. Lines, Patricia M. *Inequality in Education.* n23, p37–56, Sep 1978 (EJ 193 524; Reprint: UMI).

Safeguards provided by existing civil and criminal assault and battery laws provide inadequate protection for students. State laws (as detailed in charts and tables) provide some avenues for relief, but new legislation must be passed to ensure students' rights.

104. Corporal Punishment and Alternatives in the Schools: An Overview of Theoretical and Practical Issues. Hyman, Irwin A. et al. *Inequality in Education.* n23, p5–20, Sep 1978 (EJ 193 521; Reprint: UMI).

Many alternatives to the use of corporal punishment in the schools exist. Because the mass of survey data collected contraindicates the use of corporal punishment, the burden of proof of its effectiveness should be assumed by those who favor its use.

105. Corporal Punishment, School Suspension, and the Civil Rights of Students: An Analysis of Office for Civil Rights School Surveys. Glackman, Ted et al. *Inequality in Education.* n23, p61–65, Sep 1978 (EJ 193 526; Reprint: UMI).

Survey data from 116 schools indicate that (1) minority group students, particularly males, are corporally punished more often than their white peers; (2) boys, in general, receive more corporal punishment than girls; and (3) schools that use corporal punishment frequently also have high rates of suspension.

106. The Court's Corporal Punishment Mandate to Parents, Local Authorities, and the Profession. Englander, Meryl E. *Phi Delta Kappan.* v59, n8, p529–32, Apr 1978 (EJ 175 642; Reprint: UMI).

Reviews the position taken by the Supreme Court in supporting corporal punishment, asserts that corporal punishment is demeaning, and lists alternative approaches to the control of students.

107. The Effects of Eliminating Corporal Punishment in Schools: A Preliminary Survey. Farley, Arnold C. et al. *Inequality in Education.* n23, p57–60, Sep 1978 (EJ 193 525; Reprint: UMI).

A survey of 36 school districts indicates that there does seem to be a trend toward eliminating corporal punishment. Many districts felt that corporal punishment had proved less effective than alternative disciplinary measures such as suspension, parent conferences, counseling, and programs that helped to prevent delinquency.

108. A Further Look at Corporal Punishment. Brenton, Myron. *Today's Education.* v67, n4, p52–55, Nov-Dec 1978 (EJ 202 448; Reprint: UMI).

The pros and cons of corporal punishment as a discipline policy in the schools are discussed.

109. Paddling Doesn't Work. Koslofsky, Norman. *Clearing House.* v52, n5, p232–33, Jan 1979 (EJ 199 129; Reprint: UMI).

The call for a return to corporal punishment grows out of frustration. Students are most defiant now and authority figures are weaker and shaken. It is tempting to strike out in anger, but corporal punishment is not, and never has been, a real solution.

REPORTS

110. Delinquency, Corporal Punishment, and the Schools. Welsh, Ralph S., National Council on Crime and Delinquency, Hackensack, NJ, New-Gate Resource Center, Feb 1978, 49p; Chapter 39 of "Theoretical Perspectives on School Crime, Volume I"; Not available in hard copy due to print quality. Sponsoring agency: Department of Health, Education, and Welfare, Washington, DC (ED 158 369; Reprint: EDRS).

One of 52 theoretical papers on school crime and its relation to poverty, this chapter reports that there is a growing trend in this country to blame youth crime on parental permissiveness. Available data fail to support this and show that all types of crime, including school crime, develop within families and school systems emphasizing aversive and authoritarian discipline techniques. Also, racism and personal injustice are more common in an authoritarian atmosphere. Of all types of aversive behavior control, corporal punishment appears most apt to induce aggression. A theory relating delinquent aggression to the severity of parental discipline is sketched out, and it is suggested that a national effort be made to discourage the use of corporal punishment as a socially acceptable child-rearing technique. Since corporal punishment tends to produce both fear and anger, its continued use in the school can only be counterproductive to the learning process. A joint effort should be made to train teachers in nonaversive but effective techniques of pupil control. In addition, individual teachers need support of well-trained guidance personnel who are willing to enter homes and work with the behavioral problems at their source.

111. A Practical Defense of Corporal Punishment.
Reinholz, Lansing K. Sep 1976, 11p; Paper presented at the Annual Meeting of the American Psychological Association (84th, Washington, DC, September 3–7, 1976) (ED 132 733; Reprint: EDRS).

The author of this paper maintains that corporal punishment is a desirable alternative to permanent suspension (expulsion) in cases involving unmanageable students. There are restrictions that must be placed on the use of corporal punishment so that it is a beneficial and not a destructive force. No physical harm should be done to students. The grievant should not do the punishing. Corporal punishment should be a last resort, and students should be given the choice between it and permanent suspension. Careful records must be kept, and there should always be a witness present. Corporal punishment should be administered only once unless the undesirable behavior decreases for a period following its initial use. Teachers and administrators alike would prefer to be concerned with teaching, not with discipline. Corporal punishment can offer one way of deterring disruption of the educational process.

112. Proceedings: Conference on Corporal Punishment in the Schools: A National Debate
(Washington, DC, February 18–20, 1977). Wise, James H., Ed., Children's Hospital of the District of Columbia, Washington, DC, Feb 1977, 59p. Sponsoring agency: National Institute of Education (DHEW), Washington, DC (ED 144 185; Reprint: EDRS).

The conference from which these papers were taken was designed to present a balanced cross section of opinion on the controversial subject of corporal punishment in the school. The papers contained in this volume include a review of the research on the effects of punishment, an analysis of state legislation regulating corporal punishment in the schools, as well as papers for and against the use of corporal punishment. Special attention is given to the U.S. Supreme Court's decision in the Ingraham v. Wright case, in which the Court ruled that corporal punishment does not violate student's Eighth Amendment rights (freedom from cruel and unusual punishment) nor require due process before it is applied to students. The volume concludes with an open forum dialogue among representatives of the American Federation of Teachers, the American Psychological Association, and the National Parent Teacher Association.

113. To Punish or Not to Punish: The Administrator's Dilemma.
Wattenberg, William W., Apr 1975, 10p; Paper presented at the Annual Meeting of the American Educational Research Association (60th, Washington, DC, March 30–April 3, 1975) (ED 111 102; Reprint: EDRS).

A discussion of the political aspects of administrative decision making concerns the sanctioning or prohibiting of corporal punishment in schools in general and the action taken when teachers who use corporal punishment come under attack. The data, derived from the author's participant observation in the Detroit Public Schools, indicate that (1) corporal punishment has been an accepted and practiced control mechanism in many schools; (2) most large school systems have a machinery for protecting teachers who may be jeopardized because they have administered physical punishment; and (3) parents filing civil suits have found that both teachers and administrators have liability insurance and are represented in court by attorneys for their professional organizations. Where corporal punishment is sanctioned, educators are shielded effectively even when overzealous, ill-advised, or sadistic. The removal of that shield, the primary target in any political effort to bar corporal punishment, is the concern of the remainder of the paper.

114. Some Myths Regarding the Use of Corporal Punishment in the Schools.
Clarizio, Harvey. Apr 1975, 11p; Paper presented at the Annual Meeting of the American Educational Research Association (60th, Washington, DC, March 30–Apr 3, 1975) (ED 109 829; Reprint: EDRS).

Studies of child-rearing practices have consistently shown that the degree of physical punishment used by parents is positively correlated with various forms of psychopathology and negatively related to conscience development. One explanation of these findings has to do with modeling; the child learns by example that aggressiveness toward those of lesser power is permissible. Many educators maintain that judicious occasional use of corporal punishment is beneficial to the child. While resulting in immediate decrements in the undesired behavior, however, occasional punishment actually strengthens the behavior by allowing it to be intermittently reinforced. Unfortunately, many educators are apparently unaware that effective and more humane alternatives exist. A list of techniques for maintaining discipline without physical punishment was prepared by the National Education Association Task Force on Corporal Punishment. From the limited amount of research on the popularity of physical punishment, it appears that approximately 55–65 percent of school officials, but only one-third of parents, feel that it is an effective technique.

115. **Student Attitudes toward Corporal Punishment.*** Risner, Roy Lee, United States International University, 1975, 138p (75–20,256; Reprint: DC).

The problem of the study was to determine the attitudes of students toward corporal punishment, and its effectiveness as a disciplinary process. The study was designed to delineate those differences in attitudes attributed to age, grade, sex, ethnic group, and socioeconomic level.

The method was to conduct individual interviews with 200 students from Banning, California and Palmdale, California. The selection of students included the 1974 summer school enrollments of Coombs Intermediate School, every third student at Banning High School, every tenth student from Palmdale Intermediate School, and a Palmdale driver's education class.

The results showed that a majority of students (79 percent) were in favor of corporal punishment both at home and school. Students perceived corporal punishment as 75 percent effective.

The students interviewed were generally in favor of corporal punishment's continued use in the school (71 percent). Eighty-nine percent of the 200 students interviewed felt that corporal punishment should be used at home. A majority of students in all categories (age, grade, sex, ethnic group, and socioeconomic level) favored corporal punishment. The only exception were the 17 year olds where only 44 percent favored the use of corporal punishment at school.

Corporal punishment as perceived by the student seems to be effective. Seventy-seven percent said that experiencing corporal punishment stopped them from committing punishable acts, and 70 percent said that the threat of corporal punishment stopped them from committing punishable acts.

A majority of the students did not express resentment or anger toward either the school (88 percent), home (74 percent), or the person administering the punishment (64 percent).

According to student responses corporal punishment is more effective on girls than boys, and in general favored by more girls (83 percent) than boys (79 percent). Corporal punishment seems to become less effective and to be favored less the older a student becomes.

Students from the upper socioeconomic levels were more in favor of corporal punishment and thought it more effective than did those of the lowest socioeconomic level.

Caucasians were more favorable toward corporal punishment than any other ethnic group and corporal punishment was thought to be more effective by Caucasians than any other ethnic group. The Blacks and Mexican-Americans were equally receptive to corporal punishment. Indians were at the lower end of the acceptance level.

116. **The Supreme Court Spanking Ruling: An Issue in Debate.** Welsh, Ralph S. et al. 1976, 77p; Paper presented at the Annual Convention of the American Psychological Association (Chicago, IL April 11–14, 1976) (ED 151 664; Reprint: EDRS).

Few issues have polarized the educational community so completely as the 1975 and 1977 decisions by the U.S. Supreme Court to allow corporal punishment in the schools. The symposium reported here was organized and conducted following the 1975 decision but prior to the 1977 one. Three papers in support and three papers against the ruling were read, after which the participants debated the matter. Finally, one pro and one con participant summed up the views for each side. The supporters of the ruling view corporal punishment as an effective deterrent to misbehavior, insist that it is a necessary tool for keeping order in the classroom, and see it as an alternative to permanent suspension. They admit that corporal punishment is occasionally misused, but point to the fact that other useful tools of a civilized society are also subject to misuse. The nonsupporters of the ruling view corporal punishment as a type of legalized child abuse and are convinced that it compounds the teachers' problems by escalating anger in the child. They bolster their position by pointing out instances of abuse that have occurred in the past. Both groups agree that effective alternatives to physical discipline, coupled with teachers more adequately trained to handle disciplinary problems in the classroom, would largely remove the need for the continued future use of corporal punishment.

Suspension/Expulsion

JOURNAL ARTICLES

117. **A Case of Suspension.** Cottle, Thomas J. *National Elementary Principal.* v55, n1, p4–9, Sep–Oct 1975.

Discusses the use of disciplinary suspensions in United States public schools, emphasizing the higher suspension rate for minority children and the relationship between suspensions and dropping out of school. Presents the case history of one boy whose suspension for fighting eventually led him to quit school.

118. **Suspensions in School Discipline.** Kaeser, Susan C. *Education and Urban Society.* v11, n4, p465–84, Aug 1979.

This Cleveland, Ohio, study of school suspension includes national, state, and city data on suspension rates; correlating incidence, duration, reason for suspension, and the race and sex of the students involved. Recommendations for improving discipline and reducing suspensions are included.

REPORTS

119. A Comparison of the Effectiveness of Suspension and Expulsion Alternatives at Three Selected School Districts in the Greater Houston Area.*
Mendez, Roy, University of Houston, 1979, 201p (79–19,387; Reprint: DC).

The purpose of this study was to analyze different phases of three alternative-to-suspension programs utilized in secondary schools (grades 9–12) in the Greater Houston area. First, effectiveness of the programs was studied through the variables of improved student attendance, lack of repeat assignment, facilitation of graduation, and reduction in student alienation. Second, descriptive analysis of each of the program's components was analyzed and delineated. Third, educational and sociological variables were empirically analyzed between students assigned to alternative programs and those students not assigned. Fourth, analysis of the "Alternative-to-Suspension Practices Questionnaire," as developed by the researcher was conducted to discover prevalent practices, policies, and characteristics of programs throughout the nation, Texas, and more specifically, the Houston Gulf Coast area.

The findings resulting from the data analyses in this study were the basis for the following conclusions:

1. Students assigned to alternative-to-suspension programs when compared to the students in the control group:
   a. Possessed significantly lower reading skills.
   b. Exhibited much higher rates of absenteeism.
   c. Chose vocational courses to the same degree.
   d. Participated less in extracurricular activities in two districts and similarly in one district.
   e. Displayed a much greater tendency of not achieving graduation requirements.

2. Students in alternative-to-suspension programs:
   a. Exhibited, as measured by the Jesness Inventory test, a greater degree of manifest aggression, alienation, social maladjustment, and other personality traits which indicated tendencies toward delinquency.
   b. Did not improve their school attendance after assignment to the programs in Districts A and B; both of these districts were equally ineffective in improving school attendance.
   c. Displayed the same score on the alienation scale of the inventory.

3. Administrators in responding to the "Alternative-to-Suspension Practices Questionnaire" revealed the following information:

a. The alternative programs were perceived as being beneficial and somewhat rehabilitative.
b. Utilized practices were nonuniform in nature.
c. The size of the district was a factor in the structure of the program offered.
d. Counseling was a fundamental dimension of most programs.

The following recommendations were made based upon the results of this study and experiences of the researcher while conducting the research. Alternative programs should:

1. Serve to identify and remediate reading deficiencies as well as emotional instability.
2. Not allow students to participate in extracurricular activities if assignment is for less than ten days.
3. Have active involvement and coordination with the counseling staff.
4. Have selective assignment criteria so as to not become an administrative dumping ground for discipline cases.
5. Permit students full academic credit for work during their assignment.
6. Be articulated with a varied array of community agencies.
7. Utilize at least one professionally certified person and one or more ancilliary personnel.

120. The Effect of Suspension as a Disciplinary Technique in the Classroom of the 1970's.*
Stallworth, Robert Lee, The University of Michigan, 1977, 110p (77–26,366; Reprint: DC).

One school district in the State of Michigan served as the target area of this study. Suspension in elementary schools, junior high schools, and senior high schools was examined. Only permanent suspensions, rather than brief suspensions, were examined in this study since permanent suspensions are generally better documented than brief suspensions.

Among the findings, the following were reported: Suspension is used more often as a disciplinary technique in the junior high school than in elementary school or in senior high school. Suspension is used less often to punish infractions of school regulations and more to discipline students who engage in violent or illegal behavior. Suspension is considered a positive disciplinary measure by both teachers and administrators.

Permanent suspension was found to be a powerful disciplinary tool for educators to maintain proper control of the classroom environment. It does not appear in the school district studied that suspension is misused as a quick and arbitrary punishment for minor infractions of school regulations. Students on the whole are not lost to the educational process via suspension as it is employed in this school district since there is a policy of transfer of the student to some other school or to some alternative form of education whenever possible.

Suspension as a traditional punishment in which the student is simply rejected by the school system for a period of days or permanently is not employed in this area. The suspension technique is a positive one. The cultural shock of removing the student from his normal educational environment is employed, but followed up by counseling and replacement, hopefully quickly, to allow the student to benefit from the discipline and to develop in another environment.

121. The Relationship of Short-Term Suspension to Student Behavior in an Urban Secondary School.* Vincent, James Edward, The University of Nebraska—Lincoln, 1978, 91p (79–07,554; Reprint: DC).

This study was undertaken to examine short-term suspension and its relationship to selected variables: (1) in-school behavior of students, (2) student awareness of rules and regulations, (3) recidivistic behavior of students, (4) absences of students, (5) grades received by students, and (6) home background of students. The purpose in this study was to determine the relationship of short-term suspension practices to student behavior in an urban secondary school during a selected semester.

The procedures used to obtain this information were as follows:

1. A search of the pertinent literature was conducted concerning suspension studies and court cases.

2. For this study the following student records were reviewed: (a) suspension records, (b) behavioral records, (c) absence records, (d) grade and enrollment records, (e) census records, and (f) cumulative records.

3. An open-ended interview was constructed to provide in-depth examinations of the relationship of short-term suspension to student behavior from a random sample of 53 individuals selected from the following four groups: suspended students, nonsuspended students, teachers, and administrators.

4. A content analysis was implemented to develop and utilize the interview-record data.

5. Data from the interview and records were analyzed.

The major findings of this study were:

1. Both suspended and nonsuspended students were significantly less positive than teachers or administrators about the use of multiple short-term suspensions for violations of different rules and regulations.

2. Students who had never been suspended possessed a fear of short-term suspension. However, once a student had been suspended, loss of the controlled fear apparently resulted; and it can be concluded that repeated use of short-term suspension may have limited impact. In general, in this study, short-term suspension was seen to be of more value in the effect it had on other students than the effect it had on the student who was suspended. In contrast, short-term suspension was not seen as benefiting or helping students to change their behavior. The data from this study suggest that short-term

suspension was considered a control factor for the maintenance of an orderly school.

3. For absenteeism or academic performance (grade point averages), suspended students formed a more variant group; suspended students had a significantly higher absenteeism rate and a significantly lower grade point average than non-suspended students.

4. A comparison of students who were suspended with students who were not suspended showed significant differences in home background; when a student was not living in a home with two parents (or parent surrogates), the likelihood of disciplinary infractions leading to short-term suspension was significantly increased.

122. School Suspensions: Are They Helping Children? A Report. Washington Research Project, Cambridge, MA, Children's Defense Fund, 1975, 270p (ED 113 797; Reprint: EDRS—HC not available; also available from Children's Defense Fund, 1746 Cambridge Street, Cambridge, MA 02138).

This book examines the incidence and impact of school suspension and discusses its effectiveness as a disciplinary measure. Basically, this publication is intended to follow up and expand on a 1974 report on the use of school suspension, "Children out of School in America." Data for this current study were drawn from suspension data submitted to the federal Office for Civil Rights by 2,862 school districts, from an independent survey of over 6,500 families in nine states and the District of Columbia, and from more than 300 additional interviews with school officials and community leaders. Individual chapters offer an overview of the use of school suspension, present various educational administrators' views on school discipline, examine why children are suspended and how suspension affects them, summarize statistical data on the incidence of suspension, discuss suspension as a form of racial discrimination, describe the legal requirements for due process in suspension cases, and suggest how schools can meet those requirements, and examine various approaches that have been tried as alternatives to suspension. Numerous tables that summarize statistical data on the use of school suspension are presented throughout the book and in the appendix.

123. A Study of Attitudes towards the Use and Value of Suspension in the Urban Public School.* Bordenick, Frank Gregory, University of Pittsburgh, 1976, 109p (76–26,216; Reprint: DC).

The major focus of this study was to measure the relationship of students', teachers', parents', and administrators' attitudes toward the use and value of suspension in the urban schools and specific principles relating to suspension drawn from the literature.

In order to determine what attitudes various segments of educators, students, and parents in the urban school district have toward the use of suspension, a questionnaire with emphasis on five principles delineated from educational literature was developed, tested, and then administered. The questionnaire was administered to students, teachers, parents, and administrators in four urban public schools.

The following results and conclusions were obtained: (1) The majority of students, teachers, parents, and administrators believe suspension tends to increase respect for the teacher. (2) The majority of respondents do feel that suspension of one student, either positive or negative, has an effect on the behavior of other students. (3) A majority of respondents feel that suspension enhances the attainment of their educational objectives. (4) A majority of respondents believe that the use of suspension does have an effect, either positive or negative, on the future behavior of the student who is suspended. (5) A majority of respondents feel that the prohibited use of suspension would alter their effectiveness in the classroom. (6) The large majority of students, teachers, parents, and administrators do feel that the teachers should not have the right to administer student suspensions.

A number of recommendations for implementing the instrument and utilizing the results of the study were also suggested.

124. Suspensions and Expulsions: Current Trends in School Policies and Programs. Neill, Shirley Boes, National School Public Relations Association, Arlington, VA, 1976, 65p (ED 127 720; Reprint: EDRS—HC not available; also available from National School Public Relations Association, 1801 North Moore Street, Arlington, VA, Stock No. 411–13327).

Two 1975 Supreme Court decisions (Goss v Lopez and Wood v Strickland) have caused educators to reevaluate discipline policy in light of due process for students. Increased attention to student rights and concern for civil liberties have contributed to closer examination of suspension and expulsion in particular. School districts and state education agencies

all over the country are revamping discipline policies to provide for more alternatives to these two disciplinary measures. Good inschool suspension programs offer educational alternatives, not merely other forms of discipline. Alternative inschool suspension programs are frequently housed in separate buildings with a complete education program tailored to the individual needs of the students. This paper surveys national trends in alternatives to suspension and expulsion, as well as state and district policy changes. The positions of some professional associations (such as the National Education Association and the National Association of Secondary School Principals) toward these two controversial disciplinary measures are also presented.

125. Suspensions and Expulsions in Chicago Public Schools. Commission on Human Relations, Chicago, IL, Feb 1977, 22p (ED 167 651; Reprint: EDRS).

This report describes problems directly related to the present method of dealing with suspension and expulsion in the Chicago public schools and recommends specific strategies for dealing with these problems. Problems discussed include: (1) the need for a definition of ''gross misconduct''; (2) the need for the dissemination of information on board of education policies relative to suspension; (3) the need for thorough orientation of students as to suspendable offenses; (4) the need for clarification of suspension and expulsion policies; (5) problems related to the various roles delegated to school counselors; and (6) the loss of education experiences by suspended or expelled students. In addition, other problems that may contribute to suspensions and/or expulsions such as the socioeconomic level of students, divorce, unemployment, chronic illness, and delinquency are outlined.

Behavior Modification

JOURNAL ARTICLES

126. Behavior Change Procedures in Junior and Senior High School. Peed, Steve; Pinsker, Mark A. *Education and Urban Society.* v10, n4, p501–20, Aug 1978 (EJ 188 061; Reprint: UMI).

While behavior change procedures should not be viewed as a panacea, they do offer an attractive alternative for addressing many of the problems faced by secondary school teachers and administrators.

127. Behavior Management and Classroom Guidance in an Inner-City School. Hiltzheimer, Nancy B.; Gumaer, Jim. *Elementary School Guidance and Counseling*. v13, n4, p272–78, Apr 1979 (EJ 199 275; Reprint: UMI).

Describes how behavior management and a classroom guidance program were combined and implemented to help a fourth-grade teacher gain control of her students in an inner-city school.

128. Behavior Modification in an Elementary School: Problems and Issues. Elardo, Richard. *Phi Delta Kappan*. v59, n5, p334–38, Jan 1978 (EJ 169 847; Reprint: UMI).

Describes the implementation of a token economy as a method of controlling student behavior in an elementary school. Emphasizes student participation and discusses board issues such as teacher resistance to the program and the question of evaluation.

129. Behavioral Contracting with School Discipline Problems.* Mable, Ted John, Boston University School of Education, 1978, 104p (78–19,760; Reprint: DC).

The purpose of the study was to (1) analyze the effects of behavioral contracting upon the aversive behaviors of problem students in a school, and (2) test out a theoretical model of social integration. The model predicted that the success of a contract would be related to the degree of social integration the problem student had in his total relevant environmental field.

The method was a single-subject design utilizing a multiple-baseline technique. There were nine subjects in the study drawn from grades 6, 7, and 8. Treatment was administered to three subjects at a time after baseline had been established.

The results showed that contracting reduced the aversive target behaviors for eight of the nine subjects. Contracting also increased the on-task behavior of the subjects in the classroom, as well as improving academic performance.

Contracting is an effective tool for school administrators. The technique has a cost-beneficial value to it and helps to build rapport between the principal and the troubled youth in school. Contracting appears to be more effective with students who come from families having high social integrations, i.e., good interactive patterns with family, school, and peers, than with those of low social integrations.

130. Behavioral Self-Control in Classroom Settings: A Review of the Literature. Workman, Edward A.; Hector, Mark A. *Journal of School Psychology*. v16, n3, p227–36, Feb 1978 (EJ 188 392; Reprint: UMI).

Reviews the research on the use of behavioral self-control procedures with students in classroom settings. The use of behavioral self-control procedures appears promising with on-task and academic behaviors and inconclusive with disruptive behavior.

131. Self-Control in the Classroom. McLaughlin, T. F. *Review of Educational Research*. v46, n4, p631–63, Fall ~~Feb~~ 1976.

This review is divided into four categories which reflect different uses of self-control procedures in classroom research: (1) application of various components of self-control as an intervention procedure; (2) use of self-control procedures to maintain behavior already under the control of systematic reinforcement procedures; (3) evaluation of self-control as compared with other intervention procedures; and (4) examination of variables that appear to be related to the effectiveness of self-control.

Alternative Programs/Innovative Practices

JOURNAL ARTICLES

132. Advocacy Groups and School Discipline. Haralson, Eric. *Education and Urban Society*. v11, n4, p527–46, Aug 1979.

This report deals with the school advocacy group, which hews very closely to the "traditional" advocacy concept in championing the cause of schoolchildren and their parents. The explicit focus here is on the groups' activities in the area of school discipline.

133. Alternative Classroom for Disruptive Students.
Rakowsky, Stanley G. *NASSP Bulletin*. v63,
n425, p122–23, Mar 1979.

Described is a no-nonsense approach toward discipline
—a highly structured, regimented alternative classroom
which is the last resort of students facing expulsion.

134. Ask the Public for Discipline Help. Sharpes,
Donald K. *The American School Board Journal*.
v166, n10, p30, Oct 1979.

Described is a program whereby school officials,
parents, and community agencies work together to reduce
school discipline problems.

135. Behavioral Teacher. Sklarz, D. P. *Clearing
House*. v52, n9, p429–30, May 1979 (EJ 202 538;
Reprint: UMI).

A junior high school principal describes how his teachers
participate in the discipline process. They share duty in a
small room and act as a behavioral teacher, using a Glasser
reality-oriented approach. Mildly disruptive pupils are sent
to the behavioral teacher instead of to the assistant principal.

136. Building Discipline in a "Tough" School.
Macekura, Joseph. *Social Education*. v42, n2,
p100–04, Feb 1978 (EJ 174 505; Reprint: UMI).

Describes methods adopted by a junior high school
in Virginia to ease racial tensions following a desegregation
decree in 1965. Methods included in-service programs for
teachers, human relations workshops for students and teachers,
development of special learning opportunities, and school-
community interaction.

137. But Student Committees Can Cut Peer Violence.
Arnhart, Warren N.; Duranceau, Jack L. *American
School Board Journal*. v166, n1, p36–37, Jan 1979
(EJ 194 040; Reprint: UMI).

This program's success is based on trust between the
committee members and the administration, the administration's willingness to share power with students—some of
whom have not been model students, and the selection of
students who are "underground" leaders and who are willing
and able to help resolve student conflicts.

**138. Competency-Based Approach to Discipline—
It's Assertive.** Canter, Lee. *Thrust for Educational
Leadership*. v8, n3, p11–13, Jan 1979.

Assertive Discipline (AD) advocates a systematic
approach which enables teachers to set firm, consistent limits
for students while remaining cognizant of students' needs for
warmth and positive support. This article describes effective

and ineffective teacher disciplinary behaviors, AD compe-
tencies, and the implementation of AD at Rice Elementary
School.

**139. The COOL Connection: Alternative to Sus-
pension.** West, Edwin L. et al. *Middle School
Journal*. v9, n1, p10–11, Nov 1978 (EJ 190 422;
Reprint: UMI).

One of the major strategies utilized to address the problem
of suspension and expulsion in High Point, North Carolina
schools was the establishment of alternative learning centers
in each junior high school.

140. COPE: An Alternative to School Suspension.
Boyle, Thomas J. *Catalyst for Change*. v5, n2,
p12–15, Win 1979.

The COPE program, instituted in the North Allegheny
School system in 1974, is an in-school suspension program
that utilizes a counseling approach aimed at reducing con-
formity to deviant peer norms while encouraging the display
of acceptable behavior in the school setting. During one year,
93 percent of COPE students returned to and remained in
their regular classrooms without further violations of school
norms. This report describes COPE's program objectives,
staff roles, and community linkages.

141. The Crises-Intervention Teacher. Morse,
William C. *Today's Education*. v64, n2, p62–63,
Mar–Apr 1975.

Some schools are providing teachers with a special
resource coteacher to provide crisis intervention services
for pupils when their coping capacity begins to fall apart.

**142. The Elimination of Discipline Problems through
a Combined School-Home Motivational System.**
Ayllon, Teodoro et al. *Behavior Therapy*. v6, n5,
p616–26, Oct 1975.

Using a classroom of Black third graders, the effect of
school/home cooperation in discipline was studied. Parents
were instructed to provide differential consequences if their
child did or did not come home with a daily "good conduct"
letter from the teacher. It was concluded that this type of
reinforcement system was effective in reducing disruptive
classroom behavior.

143. Establishing Centers for Conflict Resolution.
Sartore, Richard. *Elementary School Guidance
and Counseling*. v11, n4, p300–01, Apr 1977.

The creation of "areas" designed for conflict resolution
has been an effective method of teaching important communication skills. Elementary youngsters (K–6) who may be at odds
with one another are placed in a situation that is conducive to

generating face-to-face interaction. The location of "conflict areas" should be strategically chosen, relatively quiet and private. Referrals are received from staff members, parents and other students.

144. The Gentle Art of Classroom Discipline. Jones, Frederic H. *National Elementary Principal*. v58, n4, p26–32, Jun 1979 (EJ 203 096; Reprint: UMI).

Gives a general introduction to the Classroom Management Training Program (Santa Cruz, California) approach to maintaining discipline in the classroom and provides more extensive discussion of three aspects of the method—limit setting, the incentive system, and instructional techniques.

145. Helping the Middle School Student in Trouble. Duff, Charles F. *NASSP Bulletin*. v63, n24, p50–54, Feb 1979 (EJ 196 056; Reprint: UMI).

Describes a group approach with parents, teachers, and students, which worked in helping students who have problems in school.

146. How Peoria Slashed Its Expulsion Rate and Eased Its Discipline Problems, Too. Burdette, D. George. *American School Board Journal*. v165, n5, p37, May 1978 (EJ 177 708; Reprint: UMI).

A student recommended for expulsion may, under certain circumstances, enter into a period of probation instead.

147. Improving Learning through Peer Leadership. Johnson, Claradine et al. *Phi Delta Kappan*. v59, n8, p560, Apr 1978 (EJ 175 654; Reprint: UMI).

The Peer Leadership Program decreased student absences, the dropout rate, physical attacks, and vandalism costs, and increased student involvement.

148. In-School Suspension: No Panacea, but the Impact is Positive. White, Brian. *Phi Delta Kappan*. v58, n6, p497–98, Feb 1977.

The vice-principal of Knoxville Junior High School in Pittsburgh describes the merits and problems of his school's Learning Adjustment Center, a structured classroom for suspended students.

149. Meet Charles Head. *Today's Education*. v68, n4, p54–58, Sep–Oct 1979.

Charles Head discusses, in an interview, the discipline committee at Dallas' Hillcrest High School. The committee uses a group counseling approach.

150. A Middle School's Plan for an After-School Detention Program. Scott, William C. *NASSP Bulletin*. v63, n424, p55–58, Feb 1979 (EJ 196 057; Reprint: UMI).

An after-school detention program was developed to help students increase their self-awareness, to understand and respect the rights of others, and to increase their ability to relate to their peers, teachers, and other adults.

151. Mr. Glasser's Gentle Rod. Lipman, Victor. *American Education*. v14, n7, p28–31, Aug–Sep 1978 (EJ 200 758; Reprint: UMI).

The author describes and gives examples (from Boston schools) of a nonpunitive approach to classroom discipline designed by William Glasser. The Glasser approach involves getting the student to make a commitment to change his undesirable behavior through class communications.

152. Options in High School Discipline. Sinner, Gregg; Sinner, J. L. *Phi Delta Kappan*. v59, n6, p407–09, Feb 1978 (EJ 171 609; Reprint: UMI).

Describes seven alternatives to the traditional offerings in one high school. These programs are designed to counteract student boredom, frustration, anxiety, and related causes of discipline problems.

153. A Preventive Approach to School Violence and Vandalism: An Experimental Study. Mayer, G. Roy; Butterworth, Tom W. *Personnel and Guidance Journal*. v57, n9, p436–41, May 1979 (EJ 200 919; Reprint: UMI).

The investigators attempted to employ strategies that would attack identified perpetrators of school violence and vandalism existing within schools. Results indicated that the dollar costs of vandalism and frequency of inappropriate student behavior decreased more in experimental than in control schools.

154. The Problem Fighters. Bailey, Martha. *Childhood Education*. v55, n1, p25, Oct 1978 (EJ 194 763; Reprint: UMI).

Describes the role and function of the "Problem Fighters," a group of children in intermediate school (Opelika, Alabama), committed to dealing with racial tensions in the school.

155. Problems of Achieving Rehabilitation and Punishment in Special School Environments. Wiles, David K.; Rockoff, Edward. *Journal of Law and Education*. v7, n2, p65–76, Apr 1978 (EJ 177 712; Reprint: UMI).

Explores the legal implications of in-school suspension practices through consideration of individual v institutional rights within a punitive-rehabilitative setting. Discusses the applicability of the prison hospital model to schools and argues that future legal action may challenge the viability of in-school suspension practices.

156. Putting a School Back Together. Hampe, Barry. *American Education.* v15, n8, p29–30, 32–35, Oct 1979.

Four schools in Hawaii which had been plagued by violence, vandalism, and discipline problems have reduced problems significantly through the use of a team approach learned at Awareness House in Oakland, California.

157. Schools Where It Pays to Be Good. Chan, Janet. *McCall's.* v105, n12, p46, Sep 1978.

Describes programs in California, Virginia, and Florida high schools which reward students with cash or prizes when attendance improves or vandalism decreases.

158. Students Can Be Effective Change Agents. Wright, Johnny. *NASSP Bulletin.* v63, n424, p44–49, Feb 1979 (EJ 196 055; Reprint: UMI).

A student participatory model, developed to combat a drug problem, could be helpful in solving other school problems.

159. A Successful Alternative. Alderman, Terry W. *Journal of International Association of Pupil Personnel Workers.* v20, n4, p182–87, Sep 1976.

The author describes a successful counseling program as an alternative to suspension for disruptive students.

160. Two Successful Methods for Dealing with Discipline. Hudgens, John H. *NASSP Bulletin.* v63, n430, p113–14, Nov 1979.

A student supreme court and an after-school detention are two methods that a South Carolina high school has found to be successful.

161. Territory and Classroom Management: An Exploratory Case Study. Nay, W. Robert et al. *Behavior Therapy.* v7, n2, p240–46, Mar 1976.

This study of a fourth-grade class utilized territory as a reinforcer for good classroom behavior. Each student chose and marked his/her individual seating area. Violations of classroom rules meant removal from one's own territory to seating in a no man's land at the side of the room. This treatment produced reductions in both out-of-seat behavior and verbal misbehavior.

162. A Truancy Program: The Child Welfare Agency and the School. Johnson, Janis T. *Child Welfare.* v55, n8, p573–80, Sep–Oct 1976.

Through a cooperative program between the Lancaster (Pennsylvania) County Bureau of Children's Services and the public schools, truant students were diverted from the juvenile justice system and served by bureau caseworkers, who arranged conferences bringing together the truant student, his/her parents, and school personnel to define the problem and to formulate a plan to improve the student's attendance. While this conference alone solved the truancy problem in 30 percent of the cases, the caseworker was able to provide referrals if family or emotional problems still existed. This article describes the program's goals, its benefits and problems, and some of its evaluative data on reduction in truancy rates.

163. Using Negotiation to Resolve Teacher-Student Conflicts. DeCecco, John P.; Schaeffer, Gary A. *Journal of Research and Development in Education.* v11, n4, p64–77, Sum 1978.

Attempts to present reasons for using negotiation to resolve school conflicts, using a model based on the understanding of conflict and the cognitive and affective response to conflict. Describes the research upon which the model is based, how school personnel may be trained to use negotiation, and discusses briefly the relationship of negotiation and discipline.

REPORTS

164. Alternative Disciplinary Programs and Practices in Pennsylvania Schools. An Addendum to the Guidelines for School Discipline. Pennsylvania State Department of Education, Harrisburg, PA, Bureau of Instructional Support Services, Apr 1977, 70p; Prepared by the Division of Pupil Personnel Services (ED 144 246; Reprint: EDRS).

This document summarizes what disciplinary approaches other than detention, suspension, expulsion, and corporal punishment are being used in the schools of Pennsylvania. This information was obtained in a survey of selected Pennsylvania school districts. The disciplinary approaches fall into two main categories: (1) disciplinary techniques, which are single, specific activities, and (2) alternative programs, which attempt to attack the whole problem from many directions. The major disciplinary techniques listed in the survey questionnaires were punishment (including withholding privileges, isolation, and use of demerit systems), parental involvement (including home visitations, conferences with teachers, and reporting students' misconduct), individualization (including counseling and referral), adjustment of educational offerings (including schedule changes, tutoring, and special assignments), and behavior modification (including behavioral contracts and reward systems). Alternative discipline problems are varied, ranging from simple inschool suspension classes to fully developed alternative schools where students may enroll for one or more years. Summaries of alternative discipline practices in 20 Pennsylvania school districts are included.

165. Alternatives. Alternative Discipline and Suspension Program Handbook, Campbell County Junior High. Campbell County School District 1, Gillette, WY, 1979, 12p; best copy available (ED 172 460; Reprint: EDRS).

This booklet explains a program of discipline and suspension for students who come in conflict with school policy. The Alternative Discipline and Suspension Program (ADSP) operates in an environment of strict adherence to set rules where a student must earn advancement through and eventually out of ADSP back to regular classroom attendance. This booklet explains the basis of the program—accumulating points—and the four phases, which include a final phase of transition back to the classroom. Criteria listed for referral to ADSP include infractions such as theft, drug use, and truancy. Rules and regulations for the alternative program are listed, and a fill-in evaluation form is included at the end.

166. Alternatives to School Disciplinary and Suspension Problems. South Carolina State Department of Education, Columbia, Division of Instruction, Jan 1976, 32p; Prepared by the Task Force on Alternatives to School Disciplinary and Suspension Problems (ED 140 509; Reprint: EDRS).

Policies and procedures for disciplining students should be designed to teach them responsibility, rather than simply punish them. Providing educational opportunities to behavioral deviants is a problem that does not have a simple solution. However, alternatives to suspension or expulsion must be attempted before these disciplinary actions are taken. This document describes alternatives to suspension, as well as suggesting ways in which discipline problems may be reduced. The legal rights of students (including due process in suspension and expulsion cases) are described, and South Carolina's statutes governing student discipline are included.

167. Alternatives to Suspension. *The Practitioner*. Vol. III, No. 4. Stephens, Richard; Thomson, Scott, National Association of Secondary School Principals, Reston, VA, Apr 1977, 13p (ED 137 922; Reprint: EDRS—HC not available; also available from National Association of Secondary School Principals, 1904 Association Drive, Reston, VA 22091).

Court decisions that changed suspension procedures to be followed by principals have caused uncertainty about the extent of the principal's authority to discipline students. Suspension is, therefore, being increasingly viewed as a last resort. This newsletter groups alternatives to suspension into three main categories: student detention, intervention programs utilizing school resources as well as the courts and community agencies, and prevention techniques. The last section of this newsletter includes descriptions of alternatives to suspension programs developed in different high schools across the country.

168. Deinstitutionalization of Status Offenders: An In-School Suspension Project. Haussmann, Stephen E. Apr 1979, 9p; Paper presented at the Annual Internation Convention, The Council for Exceptional Children (57th, Dallas, TX, April 22–27, 1979, Session T–10) (ED 171 013; Reprint: EDRS).

The document describes the In-School Suspension Project (ISSP), a program of the Northeast High School Complex in Macon, Georgia, which assigns students to in-school or in-house suspension rooms as an alternative to suspending juvenile delinquents/offenders out of school. The remedial strategy is reported to call for the cooperation of the county juvenile court and the department of human resources-youth services authorities in using ISSP as a referral device. It is stated that, once a determination of suspension is made, a contact person for each school ensures that all classroom assignments for the student are assembled and forwarded to ISSP along with a copy of the suspension notice. Another aspect of the remedial strategy is reported to include individualized instruction for each student. Three main advantages which have resulted from the use of ISSP are listed: (1) students are counted as present in school while assigned to ISSP, and thus the schools benefit from an increased ADA; (2) as students are required to complete all assignments before release, they keep current on their regular class work and are often able to move ahead of their classmates in work completed; and (3) students in ISSP are not "on the streets" associating with other youth and thus the likelihood of their contact with juvenile offenders is decreased.

169. The Development and Implementation of a Program of Open Campus. Sandercock, James M., Jun 1976, 79p (ED 133 830; Reprint: EDRS).

The purpose of this practicum was to develop and implement a workable program of open campus for the Harriton High School of Lower Merion, Pennsylvania. The first phase of the practicum defined needs and shortcomings, defined objectives, developed a model program of open campus, and evaluated this program. In the second phase of the practicum, a refined program was implemented into the school and the open campus program was evaluated. The evaluation indicated that the model program was successful in terms of fostering student self-discipline and an atmosphere conducive to academic achievement. Also, subsystems related to the program of open campus—attendance, discipline—improved under the program developed.

170. Effects of a Glasserian-Oriented Administrator in a Non-Glasserian School on Discipline Related Problems.* Ries, Wayne Casper, Wayne State University, 1978, 160p (79–08,953; Reprint: DC).

The educator's role has changed during the past three decades largely as a result of outside societal forces. This change has left the educator less willing to become involved with the problems of the students.

At the same time, the student population has experienced changes in its value orientation that demands more involvement.

William Glasser examined the school in light of the above and found the educational institution failing to adequately meet the needs of its clientele. Glasser feels that too many students have not achieved a "success" identify. Further, he believes that these "failure" oriented students respond by exhibiting two general symptoms: either they become overtly aggressive toward school or they withdraw from the school setting.

Glasser's approach in dealing with the resulting problems is based upon a nonpsychoanalytic theory which he terms Reality Therapy. His approach to handling problems in the schools has received wide acceptance and his educator training center has helped promulgate his teachings. Central to their approach is the total school staff acceptance of the Glasserian procedure.

However, societal forces may tend to inhibit acceptance of a Glasserian approach. In this situation, could a single educator still have positive effects using a Glasserian Reality Therapy discipline procedure?

The subject of this dissertation is the examination of such a situation with respect to an administrator, responsible for the discipline of a segment of a secondary school population.

Although much of the data were not significantly different for experimental or control, trends often appeared favoring the experimental. A study done over a longer time-line may have yielded more significant results.

171. Improve Communication to Improve Behavior. Blume, Robert A.; Blume, Delorys E., Apr 1978, 15p; Paper presented at National Conference on Humanistic Education (Carrollton, GA, April 29, 1978) (ED 156 602; Reprint: EDRS).

The problem of children's misbehavior in school is an urgent concern. Although misbehavior is not unique to the school, the whole of society suffers from violence. It is important to recall that those committing crimes today were yesterday's students. There are two modes for discipline in the schools. The "established" mode aims for teacher control of children's behavior. This mode assumes that students cannot be trusted to pursue their own learning. In contrast, the "emergent" mode aims to help children assume responsibility for their behavior and to encourage them to think about the effects of their actions upon others. The underlying philosophy of the emergent mode is that human beings have a natural potential for learning. The emergent mode of discipline builds upon the ideas of Ginott, Glasser, and Gordon

which stress the importance of good student-teacher communication in preventing problems and teaching that irresponsible behavior is not acceptable. Gordon's "Teacher Effectiveness Training" is a good method for opening up student-teacher communication and for helping children accept personal responsibility for their actions. It is important for the schools to implement the emergent mode which requires children to take responsibility for their behavior so that they may become responsible citizens in a democratic society.

172. In-School Alternatives to Suspension: Conference Report. Garibaldi, Antoine M., Ed., National Institute of Education (DHEW), Washington, DC, Apr 1979, 174p (ED 173 951; Reprint: EDRS; also available from Superintendent of Documents, US Government Printing Office, Washington, DC 20402, Stock No. 017-080-020-38-6).

In April 1978 the National Institute of Education held a conference to explore alternative approaches to suspension as a disciplinary procedure. This publication reproduces the proceedings of this conference, which reflects a cross-section of opinion on alternative programs provided by panelists and speakers from many sectors of the educational community. Highlighted were such considerations as legal issues in the discipline process, effective implementation and organization of programs, and the status of discipline in public education. A presentation by Junious Williams detailed the pros and cons of alternative programs, as well as presenting recent figures on suspension and expulsion in the nation's schools. Hayes Mizell offered a discussion on components essential to implementation of inschool alternative programs. Eight directors of inschool alternative programs presented detailed descriptions of their alternative plans. The Honorable Shirley Chisholm delivered a keynote address proposing a policy among federal agencies promoting the design of more alternative education and employment programs for youth.

173. Positive Alternatives to Student Suspensions: An Overview and Attachments. Bailey, Ralph E.; Kackley, John C., All Children's Hospital, St. Petersburg, FL, 1977, 48p. Sponsoring agency: Bureau of Elementary and Secondary Education (DHEW/OE), Washington, DC (ED 165 347; Reprint: EDRS).

The prevention and resolution of student behavior problems were the goals of the Positive Alternatives to Student Suspensions (PASS) Program involving schools in Pinellas County, Florida. Workshops for staff and administrators aimed toward creating a humanized caring school. Classroom activities attempted to create situations in which students and teachers could get to know and appreciate each other. Programs for students run by a psychologist and social worker aimed at self-exploration and personal growth. Encounter groups for personnel stressed self-exploration and facilitation of positive interactions through values clarification, transactional analysis, and other applied behavioral science techniques. Parent training groups fostered open communication, sharing of concerns, problem-solving, and values clarification using techniques from parent effectiveness training, behavior modification, and transactional analysis. A "time-out room" provided a place where students could talk out personal problems before the problems became discipline problems. A "Student's School Survival Course" allowed students to receive positive feedback from teachers and other students. A "Student's Home Survival Course" used reality therapy, transactional analysis, and rational behavior therapy to help students explore positive alternatives for resolving problems at home. During the two years in which the program operated, the PASS schools had significantly fewer student suspensions than did control schools.

174. A Program to Reduce Vandalism and to Improve Student Behavior at Vineland High School North. Valentine, Charles F., Nov. 1978, 40p; Paper presented at the Annual Meeting of the National Association of Secondary School Principals (63rd, Houston, TX, February 2–6, 1979) (ED 173 899; Reprint: EDRS).

New Jersey's Vineland High School North faced many behavioral and vandalism problems during its first year of operation (1976–77) and adopted a program to improve this situation during its second year. This effort involved adoption and thorough dissemination of student rules, a series of parent orientation meetings, a new community information program, the creation of a Parent Teacher Association, an in-service program in humanistic education, a peer leadership program, and the hiring of paraprofessionals to improve communication between home and school. During the program's initial year, vandalism dropped substantially and most student behavior improved. Suspension figures were higher due to greater attention to the problems that remained. The need for police intervention was greatly reduced, although arrest levels remained near the original level. The problems, their causes, the program designed to solve them, and the results of that program are described briefly in this speech.

175. Project Student Concerns: Final Report. Jefferson County Education Consortium, Louisville, KY, June 1978, 259p; Parts of pages 138-190, statistical tables, may be marginally legible due to reproduction quality of the original document. Sponsoring agency: Office of Education (DHEW), Washington, DC (ED 159 281; Reprint: EDRS—HC not available.)

This report is concerned with the analysis and implementation of intervention strategies designed to reduce disproportionate suspensions of minority students. As the final phase of a two-phase study, this report consists of three

components: (1) continued monitoring of suspension data; (2) field studies in four Jefferson County, Kentucky, public secondary schools selected for their high and disproportionate suspension rates for Black students during the first quarter of the 1976–77 school year; and (3) implementation of four different intervention strategies in the four target schools. Field coordinators assigned to each school for the last six weeks of the 1976–77 school year helped staff to plan 1977–78 school activities based on the speccific discipline/suspension problems experienced by each school. An intervention strategy was then designed to address the needs of each target school. A complete description of the development of each strategy, the original design, evolution to the final form, and evaluation are included in the model description and evaluation sections of this report. The four field study cases are presented in order to provide a frame of reference for understanding the individual school setting into which each model was introduced.

176. A Proposal for an Alternative to Out-of-School Suspension for Worthington High School Students: The Saturday School. Gooding, James; Fitsko, Michael. Nov 1978, 24p (ED 169 603; Reprint: EDRS).

It is proposed that a disciplinary Saturday school may be a good alternative to student suspension because it solves many of the problems involved with suspending students from school. Allowing students to attend Saturday school rather than being suspended gives them an opportunity to improve their grades and to attend all their regular classes. It avoids the stigma of absence from school and does not reward those skipping school with the opportunity to miss more classes. Problems with the program include transportation and interference with students' Saturday jobs. The program would allow those who cooperate fully with Saturday school activities to leave early or reduce their attendance days. Evaluation by parents, students, and teachers is an important component of the program. The major cost for the program is for the supervision and instruction of students. Teachers, honor students, or resource persons may be utilized as supervisors. Attachments to the document include forms used in the Saturday school program and an evaluation of the program.

177. A Rationale and Model for the Training of Educational Specialists to Work with Disruptive Youth. Bell, Raymond; Semmel, Elizabeth, National Council on Crime and Delinquency, Hackensack, NJ, NewGate Resource Center, Feb 1978, 33p; Chapter 3 of "Theoretical Perspectives on School Crime, Volume I" Sponsoring agency: Department of Health, Education, and Welfare, Washington, DC (ED 155 818; Reprint: EDRS).

One of 52 theoretical papers on school crime and its relation to poverty, this chapter addresses itself to the identification and training of appropriate personnel to implement intervention programs that prevent disruptive, delinquent acts within communities in general and schools in particular. Two models are presented to prepare teachers both to deal effectively with disruptive behavior and to increase the academic skills of the student who exhibits such behavior. The first model is a preservice model that can be implemented at the state level and may be used in the training of crisis-intervention "specialists." The second model is a local inservice model that can be introduced into a local school system involving available personnel.

178. Schools without Failure— 1977. Glasser's Approach to Discipline— Realistic and Working. Glasser, William. Feb 1977, 17p; Paper presented at the Annual Meeting of the American Association of School Administrators (109th, Las Vegas, NV, February 25–28, 1977) (ED 137 958; Reprint: EDRS).

Glasser presents the ten-step approach to school discipline based on his concept of Reality Therapy, discusses preliminary results of implementation of this approach, and then presents the results of a recent survey. Surveyed were 24 schools— 14 elementary, 5 junior high schools, and 5 high schools—chosen to give a representative picture of education in this country. Summative statements of each of the 11 questions are presented. The questions deal with the success of the method, the changes each school made in the approach, and the effects the program had on the school.

179. A Study to Determine the Effectiveness of a Positive Approach to Discipline System for Classroom Management.* Allen, Sherwin Aaron, North Texas State University, 1978, 128p (79-11,061; Reprint: DC).

This study reports on an investigation of the effectiveness the "Postive Approach to Discipline" (PAD) system for classroom management.

The subjects for this study were teachers and students located in a middle school in a large, urban school district. Data were collected on the number of students referred to administration during ten weeks of the first quarter; the same teachers participated in a four-day workshop on the concepts and techniques of the PAD system. The teachers agreed to participate in ten follow-up sessions. Data were collected on the number of students referred to administration during ten weeks of the second quarter. The PAD system and follow-up sessions were discontinued at the end of the second quarter. Data were collected on the number of students referred to administration during ten weeks of the third quarter. The mean scores were compared on the number of students referred to administration during first quarter, second quarter, and third quarter.

Data were collected on the racial background of the students referred to administration during first quarter, second quarter, and third quarter. Mean scores on the racial background of students referred to administration were compared during first quarter, second quarter, and third quarter.

Data were collected on the 21 students most frequently referred to administration to determine the number of times corporal punishment was administered to these students. The mean scores were compared on the number of times corporal punishment was administered during ten weeks of the first quarter, ten weeks of the second quarter, and ten weeks of the third quarter.

Data were also collected for the 21 students most frequently referred to administration for the number of times they were suspended from school. The mean scores were compared on the number of suspensions from school for ten weeks of the first quarter, ten weeks of the second quarter, and ten weeks of the third quarter.

The data from the study were analyzed by the analysis of variance with repeated measures. The data indicate several implications for the utilization of the PAD system for classroom management: 1) teachers utilizing the PAD system significantly reduced the number of students referred to administration; 2) teachers utilizing the PAD system significantly reduced the number of Black students referred to administration; and 3) the PAD system was effective in reducing the number of students suspended from school.

180. Values Clarification as a Discipline Alternative for the Middle School.* Dye, Joan Converse, The University of Florida, 1979, 123p (79-21,924; Reprint: DC).

The problem of this study was to use the Gordon Personal Profile in identifying students who might become disciplinary problems and to assess the use of values clarification self-study exercises of the type first introduced by Sidney Simon in the treatment and possible prevention of disciplinary problems.

Subjects for the study were 2,105 male and female students in grades 8 and 9 of two double-session junior high schools in Hillsborough County, Florida. All subjects were given the Gordon Personal Profile during the first full week of school in the 1977–78 school year and their scores on that test were correlated with their frequency of referral to an administrator for disciplinary action the same year. The use of the scores on the Gordon Personal Profile with sex added as a variable permitted the correct classification of 88 percent of the cases in the study. This effect was significant.

The 45 students in each of the two selected schools with the greatest number of referrals to an administrator for disciplinary action for the 1976–77 school year were randomly assigned to one of the three treatment groups. One group received treatment with the values/self-study packet, "A Guide to the Study of Me," in an individually guided manner. Another group received treatment with the same values/self-study packet in a small group setting. The third group received no treatment and served as a control. Sixty of the original 90 subjects were in attendance at the close of the study. There was no significant difference in the frequency of referral for those students who received the treatment individually, those who received the treatment as a group, and those who received no treatment.

It was concluded that exposure to values clarification and self-study did not reduce the frequency of referral to an administrator for disciplinary action. It was also concluded that the Gordon Personal Profile can be used to identify violators of school policy prior to their referral for disciplinary action as a result of violating that policy.

BOOKS

181. Alternatives to Suspension. Columbia, SC: American Friends Service Committee, 1975, 31p.

The purpose of this handbook is to stimulate thought, planning, and action. Although few of the alternatives outlined here are "canned" techniques that can be readily applied, the experiences and techniques reported should stimulate the thinking of school officials and citizens so that efforts can be initiated to develop and put into practice alternatives to most suspensions. Readers are cautioned that the results of the programs and techniques have not been validated nor has their effectiveness been proven. How the alternatives work depends to a great degree on how they are executed, how relevant they are to the local situation, and how conscientiously they are implemented. Much of this handbook is made up of statements from South Carolina school superintendents that indicate what their school districts are doing to cut down on the number of out-of-school suspensions. These responses are of interest because they reflect the attitudes and philosphies of the various superintendents, as well as indicating something about their discipline programs.

182. Assertive Discipline: A Take Charge Approach for Today's Educator. Canter, Lee. Los Angeles: Canter and Associates, Inc., 1976, 190p.

Assertive discipline will help improve classroom discipline. It is a competency-based approach and will provide the skills and confidence needed to "take charge" in the classroom given the reality of today's schools. This approach does not advocate unduly harsh treatment. What it does advocate is setting firm consistent limits for the students while remaining cognizant of the reality of the student's need for warmth and positive support.

183. T.E.T. Teacher Effectiveness Training. Gordon, Thomas. New York: Longman, 1974, 366p.

This book presents guidelines for improving communication between teachers and students, as a way of creating a better learning environment. Dialogues from Gordon's Teacher Effectiveness Training Workshops are used to illustrate successful and unsuccessful communication methods. The technique of active listening is proposed for fostering effective subject matter class discussions, for motivating students to new situations, and for defusing emotions caused by disruptive events. Other sections of this book discuss modifying the classroom environment and the "no-lose" method of conflict resolution, which entails active listening and teacher/student participation in a six-step problem solving process.

Classroom Management and Discipline: Practical Guidelines for Teachers

JOURNAL ARTICLES

184. Alternatives for Breaking the "Discipline Barrier" in Our Schools. Havis, Andrew Lee. *Education*. v96, n2, p124–28, Win 1975.

Teacher tension contributes to ineffectual classroom management. Slowing down reaction to disruptive behavior in the classroom helps. Also suggested are ideas for classroom organization and modeling good behavior.

185. An Approach to Classroom Control. Cheek, V. P. S. *Visual Education*. p18–23, Oct 1977 (EJ 174 009; Reprint: UMI).

An action guide to help teachers diagnose and remedy problems of classroom misbehavior is presented through a brief discussion and a detailed flow chart.

186. Behavioral Blockbusters. Carberry, Hugh. *Instructor*. v88, n8, p73–74, 76, 78, Mar 1979 (EJ 199 919; Reprint: UMI).

A psychologist provides helpful suggestions for teachers having trouble with negativistic, impulsive, passive-dependent, and anxious children.

187. Better Discipline for Middle School Students. Johnson, Simon O. *Clearing House*. v53, n2, p86–89, Oct 1979.

These suggestions for improving the climate in the classroom have been tried and proven successful for teachers and administrators. They include ideas on administrator leadership, classroom organization, classroom principles, and identification of disruptive students.

188. Classroom Conduct Theory into Practice System. Snider, Sarah J.; Cooper, Leo J. *Action in Teacher Education*. v1, n2, p47–53, Fall–Win 1978 (EJ 197 176; Reprint: UMI).

Systematic analysis of classroom disruption and discipline problems can frequently correct undesirable behavior. The approach presented uses outside observers to help analyze problems and construct solutions.

189. Classroom Control. Bethel, Lowell J.; George, Kenneth D. *Science and Children*. v16, n5, p24–25, Feb 1979 (EJ 200 129; Reprint: UMI).

Presents basic guidelines for classroom control and discipline for teachers using new science programs that encourage independent study and hands-on activities.

190. Classroom Discipline Problems? Fifteen Humane Solutions. Hipple, Marjorie L. *Childhood Education*. v54, n4, p183–87, Feb 1978 (EJ 174 133; Reprint: UMI).

The approaches to effective discipline presented are based on knowledge of child development and learning theories. They are suggestions, not prescriptive cure-alls.

191. Classroom Management: A Microcosm of Good Government. DeNitto, John F.; Gufford, Joseph L., Jr. *Clearing House*. v52, n6, p263–64, Feb 1979 (EJ 199 136; Reprint: UMI).

The goal of classroom management, like government, is to create and maintain an environment which protects and advances individuals. Creating such a classroom environment involves trust between teacher and students, a conviction that misbehavior is relative, and student participation in finding alternatives for disruptive conduct.

192. Classroom Management: A Model. O'Bruba, William; Camplese, Donald A. *Early Years*. v10, n3, p55–6, Nov 1979.

One of the first considerations in managing classroom conditions is to identify those behaviors that need changing.

This five-step procedure includes identifying the behaviors, charting their frequency, setting goals for modification, outlining treatment, and evaluating the results.

193. Classroom Management: A Rule Establishment and Enforcemment Model. Buckley, Pamela K.; Cooper, James M. *Elementary School Journal*. v78, n4, p254–63, Mar 1978 (EJ 182 010; Reprint: UMI).

Describes a model for effective classroom management consisting of two major parts: teacher behaviors related to rule establishment and teacher behaviors related to rule enforcement. Eight categories of teacher behavior related to rule enforcement are briefly discussed.

194. Classroom Motivation and Discipline. Suessmuth, Patrick. *Elements of Technology*. v7, n4, p16–19, Win 1977–78.

The article lists and ranks in order of importance 144 motivation-discipline factors as established in William Gary Ward's 1974 survey of more than 100 technical instructors and teacher educators. Included are five factor-ranking worksheets for readers to use in comparing their thoughts on motivation-discipline with those of the survey respondents.

195. Creating Effective Classroom Discipline. Morris, Robert C. *Clearing House*. v52, n3, p122–24, Nov 1978 (EJ 195 608; Reprint: UMI).

Thirteen suggestions are made to the teacher on the establishment of classroom control; the use of various methods of punishment, including grades and extra homework; and ways of dealing with recurrent behavior problems.

196. Curbing Discipline Problems through Physical Education. Taylor, John L. *Journal of Physical Education and Recreation*. v49, n2, p38, Feb 1978.

A summary is presented of teacher suggestions for a preventive physical education program developed from a summer workshop of teachers concerned with student discipline problems.

197. Dealing with Disruptive Behavior. Schaible, A. E.; McCracken, J. David. *Agricultural Education*. v52, n2, p39, Aug 1979.

Fifty vocational agriculture classes were observed to test an instrument on disruptive behavior. Verbalizations seemed to cause the most problems (whispering, making noise, smart remarks). Suggestions are given for reducing classroom disruptions of this type.

198. Dealing with Student Misbehavior—Eclectic Review. Glickman, Carl D.; Wolfgang, Charles H. *Journal of Teacher Education*. v30, n3, p7–13, May–June 1979.

To help teachers adapt their approach to discipline to the variety of student personalities with which they must deal, the author reviews different styles and theories of discipline.

199. Developing a Lesson Plan for Classroom Discipline. Kelley, Edgar A. *Action in Teacher Education*. v1, n2, p41–45, Fall–Win 1978 (EJ 197 175; Reprint: UMI).

Preventing classroom discipline problems requires planning and a willingness to seriously examine and change regularized classroom and school policies and procedures. Specific, practical steps to provide teachers with more control in a positive learning environment are offered.

200. Discipline. Rudman, Masha K. *Instructor*. v86, n1, p67, Aug–Sep 1976.

Adult intervention is sometimes required to maintain order in the classroom. Suggestions are given for calling the class to order and dealing with an individual student who is causing a problem. Ten important overall considerations such as establishing routines and listing classroom rules are provided.

201. Discipline . . . Just Another One of the Basics. McDaniel, Thomas. *Early Years*. v10, n2, p78, 84, Oct 1979.

Discipline is not automatic; it cannot be assumed or demanded. Behavioral skills can be taught to young children like any other basic. A series of steps are presented for teaching a given behavior.

202. Discipline: You Can Do It! Canter, Lee. *Instructor*. v89, n2, p106–08, 110, 112, Sep 1979.

Assertive discipline is the subject of this guide for teachers. Competency skills guidelines are presented which research and experience indicate must be followed to deal assertively with student behavior.

203. Discipline and the High School Teacher. Thompson, George. *Clearing House*. v49, n9, p408–13, May 1976.

Develops a theory of discipline that assumes that there are certain commonalities among disciplinary situations that transcend any specific discipline problem and that the ultimate goal of any disciplinary approach should be the development within the individual pupils of a kind of self-discipline.

204. Discipline in the Secondary Classroom.
Eckbreth, Cathy. *Social Education*. v42, n2, p109–12, Feb 1978 (EJ 174 507; Reprint: UMI).

Offers suggestions to junior high school teachers regarding discipline policy. Suggestions are: explain basic rules during the first weeks of school; vary teaching techniques to avoid boredom; deal with disciplinary problems as they arise; and demonstrate personal interest in students whenever possible.

205. Do You Referee When You Really Want to Teach? *Instructor*. v86, n6, p54–58, Feb 1977.

Topics considered in this student-centered classroom workshop include workshop organization, getting to know each other, personal affirmation, cooperation, communication, and conflict resolution. Games and activities are suggested for each workshop section.

206. Don't Let Them Take You to the Barn. Hanny, Robert J. *Clearing House*. v52, n4, p152–53, Dec 1978 (EJ 199 104; Reprint: UMI).

The author advises teachers on ways to alter their own attitudes and behavior so as to improve classroom discipline and prevent students from taking advantage of them.

207. The "Guaranteed" Behavior Improvement Plan. Di Giulio, Robert. *Teacher*. v95, n8, p22–26, Apr 1978 (EJ 184, 373; Reprint: UMI).

Suggest that there is no rule that guarantees appropriate classroom behavior, yet, to control the class, a teacher must control himself. Gives 13 tenets for helping elementary teachers to maintain a controlled classroom and 12 guides for improving student behavior.

208. Guide to Sanity Saving Discipline. *Instructor*. v88, n4, p59–61, Nov 1978 (EJ 190 978; Reprint: UMI).

Describes seven detailed approaches to effective classroom discipline including: teacher assertiveness training, effective limit setting, priority problems approach, those games kids play, the eye-contact method, the paradox response, and the use of letters to parents as a discipline device.

209. How Do You Feel about Discipline? Glickman, Carl; Tamashiro, Roy. *Early Years*. v10, n3, p60–61, Nov 1979.

Presents a "Beliefs on Discipline Inventory" to help teachers clarify their own feelings on discipline and match these to specific strategies.

210. How to Cope in the Middle School Jungle. Rathbun, Dorothy. *Learning*. v6, n3, p46–47,100, Nov 1977 (EJ 176 427; Reprint: UMI).

Practical classroom management techniques are offered for secondary school teachers' daily use. The ideas emphasize presenting yourself as an adult and remaining "in charge."

211. Improving Classroom Management: A Systematic Application of Dreikurs' Theory of Misbehavior in the Elementary School. Trumble, L. Deane; Thurston, Paul. *Planning and Changing*. v7, n2, p29–34, Sum 1976.

Presents a theoretical framework developed by Rudolf Dreikurs in tabular form that can be easily used in suggesting appropriate action for a particular type of misbehavior.

212. The Individualization of Discipline for Behavior Disordered Pupils. Leviton, Harvey S. *Psychology in the Schools*. v13, n4, p445–48, Oct 1976.

This paper presents a case for the need to individualize discipline as well as instruction. The selected review of the literature indicates that published information on classroom management currently does not provide such an individualized approach. This article presents one such individualized disciplinary approach for different types of behavior disordered children.

213. Logical Consequences: A Key to the Reduction of Disciplinary Problems. Dinkmeyer, Don; Dinkmeyer, Don, Jr. *Phi Delta Kappan*. v57, n10, p664–66, June 1976.

By understanding the purpose of a student's misbehavior, letting him experience the logical consequences of his actions, letting him choose, and getting a commitment to an alternative action, the disciplinary process can systematically modify purposes and create responsible students.

214. Managing Inappropriate Behaviors. Lovitt, Thomas C. *Teachers*. v95, n5, p81–82, Jan 1978 (EJ 180 706; Reprint: UMI).

Although certain disruptive behaviors of handicapped children may have changed when they were in special classes, some of these behaviors may reappear when the students return to regular classes. Some suggestions for ways to establish and maintain peaceful situations in the classroom are presented.

215. "O.K. Kids, Let's Quiet Down." Weber, Alan. *Teacher Educator*. v13, n2, p28–32, Feb 1977 (EJ 174 575; Reprint: UMI).

The author offers suggestions of ways in which student or beginning teachers may gain class attention and hold the floor while still maintaining a positive teacher image.

216. Punishment: A Reaffirmation. Gaddis, R. G. *Clearing House*. v52, n1, p5–6, Sep 1978 (EJ 191 753; Reprint: UMI).

In the best of conceivable worlds, the use of punishment would not be necessary. In the real world of school, however, punishment is sometimes needed. The author provides guidelines for maximizing the positive effects of punishment.

217. Re Discipline: An Ounce of Prevention. Fontein, Hazel. *Social Education*. v42, n2, p105–08, Feb 1978 (EJ 174 506; Reprint: UMI).

Maintains that most discipline problems arise when students are asked to perform beyond their capabilities. Outlines several techniques for teaching social studies to slow learners. Techniques involve students in group reading, simulations, globe and map drills, neighborhood surveys, and art projects.

218. Teaching and Discipline. Teeter, Thomas A.; Teeter, Charles R. *High School Journal*. v63, n1, p12–16, Oct 1979.

This review on discipline in the secondary classroom briefly considers effective classroom management, guidelines on creating a productive classroom environment, and behavior management strategies.

219. Teaching Self-Discipline: An In-Service Model. Dobson, Judith E.; Dobson, Russell L. *Humanist Education*. v17, n4, p172–81, Jun 1979 (EJ 204 210; Reprint: UMI).

This workshop outlines various approaches of helping teach self-discipline in the classroom. These approaches provide practical suggestions for teachers. If the social environment of the school seems to be less than democratic, perhaps this workshop content, when implemented, will provide for more open, honest communication and cooperation.

220. Ten Better Ways to Classroom Management. Welch, Frances C.; Halfacre, John D. *Teacher*. v96, n2, p86–87, Oct 1978 (EJ 195 643; Reprint: UMI).

The ten basic ideas that are common to several current classroom management systems are presented. All of the suggestions are presented as alternatives to physical punishment.

221. Ten Steps to Good Discipline. Glasser, William. *Today's Education*. v66, n4, p61–63, Nov–Dec 1977.

A sequential program is outlined for improving the behavior of students in school.

222. Using Time-Out Procedures with Disruptive Students. Grayson, M. Catherine et al. *Pointer*. v24, n1, p74–81, Fall 1979.

The use of time-out has been a major technique for responding to disruptive behavior in the classroom. However, teachers have not always been clear about the procedures or purposes of the time-out method they employ. In this article, the authors discuss three different approaches to time-out: behavioral, cooling-off, and modified. Examples of each approach are provided, and critical steps common to all approaches are identified.

223. What Beginning English Teachers Need to Know about Classroom Discipline. Voth, John. *English Education*. v10, n4, p252–56, May 1979 (EJ 204 581; Reprint: UMI).

Considers classroom discipline from the standpoints of professional action v reaction, social equality v hierarchical relationships, and personal need v common needs. A bibliography is included.

224. What to Do When You See Red. Shearburn, Dudley. *Teacher*. v95, n1, p90–91, Sep 1977 (EJ 170 926; Reprint: UMI).

Describes ten affirmative actions, with suggestions on how to implement them, for handling behavior and learning problems in the classroom.

225. What You Already Know about Discipline. Burch, Noel. *NJEA Review*. v52, n2, p21–22, Oct 1978 (EJ 197 364; Reprint: UMI).

Teachers can learn to describe unacceptable student behavior, without judging it, and to define classroom conflicts as problems to be solved, not battles to be won. Two studies demonstrate that this type of democratic classroom environment decreases misbehavior and absenteeism.

226. When Kids Clash. Wolfgang, Charles H. *Early Years*. v9, n8, p52,54, Apr 1979.

The purpose of this article is to give teachers a workable process for intervening in a preschool conflict with a gradual use of power techniques.

REPORTS

227. Behavior Modification. What Research Says to the Teacher. Presbie, Robert J.; Brown, Paul L., National Education Association, Washington, DC, 1976, 39p (ED 118 563; Reprint: EDRS— HC not available; also available from NEA Publications, Order Department, The Academic Building, Saw Mill Road, West Haven, CT 06516, Stock No. 1035-3-00).

This report reviews some of the most relevant findings from the extensive research which has been done on behavior modification. It summarizes the more important, practical, concrete, and classroom-tested procedures which research shows to be effective in improving students' academic and social behaviors. The first section of the report begins by stating that a more descriptive name for the behavioral approach is behavior improvement. Next is an explanation of how consequences may be used to improve classroom behaviors. Reinforcement and punishment are discussed, as are ways to change and improve academic and social behaviors. The next section talks about the methodology of using behavior modification procedures. It contains information on pinpointing behaviors and counting and charting behaviors. Behavior modification change procedures are the topic of the third section. Discussed in this section are change procedures, modeling as a change procedure, social reinforcement procedures, activity reinforcement procedures, token reinforcement procedures, and punishment procedures. The final section suggests ways in which the reader might learn more about behavior modification. The report also contains a list of 100 selected references.

228. Classroom Discipline: Case Studies and Viewpoints. Kohut, Sylvester, Jr.; Range, Dale G., National Education Association, Washington, DC, 1979, 113p (ED 163 666; Reprint: EDRS— HC not available; also available from NEA Publications Order Department, Academic Building, Sawmill Road, West Haven, CT 06516).

This guide is designed for both preservice and inservice teachers concerned about classroom management and discipline as they relate to learning. The case studies and illustrations included are actual real-life situations observed, recorded, documented, and contributed by teachers, administrators, and paraprofessionals throughout the country in kindergarten through senior high school. The case studies represent problems and issues common to urban, suburban, and rural school districts and school personnel. Possible solutions to problems are offered, although no single best course of action is insisted upon. Theory and research findings that relate to classroom discipline are also included. The basic purpose of the text is to provide a practical guide for understanding and improving classroom communication in order to improve discipline.

229. Classroom Management: Implications for Supervision. Garza, Gonzalo. Mar 1977, 16p; Paper presented at the Annual Meeting of the Association for Supervision and Curriculum Development (32nd, Houston, TX, March 19–23, 1977) (ED 141 879; Reprint: EDRS).

Classroom management may be the most fundamental and most difficult task the teacher performs. A search of the literature reveals at least five rather different definitions of classroom management that represent particular philosophi-

cal approaches: (1) the authoritarian approach, (2) the permissive approach, (3) the behavior modification approach, (4) the approach based on creating a positive social and emotional climate in the classroom, and (5) the approach that views the classroom as a social system in which group processes are of major importance. Each of the last three represents a different but defensible position concerning classroom management, and supervisiors should encourage teachers to develop a pluralistic definition of classroom management. A sixth approach is the "bag of tricks" approach, which consists of a combination of common sense, old wives' tales, and folklore. Because this approach is not derived from a well-conceptualized base, it lacks consistency and tends to be reactive, instead of proactive. It is important that a teacher learn to identify his/her classroom management approach and be able to distinguish between instructional problems requiring instructional solutions and managerial problems requiring managerial solutions.

230. Discipline and Learning: An Inquiry into Student-Teacher Relationships. National Education Association, Washington, DC, 1975, 129p (ED 103 968; Reprint: EDRS— HC not available; also available from NEA Order Department, The Academic Building, Saw Mill Road, West Haven, CT 06516, Stock No. 1349-2-00).

Learning can only take place in an environment that reflects the teacher's care for all the students; that care includes the establishment and maintenance of good discipline. This book approaches the general topic of discipline from a historical perspective and from a contemporary point of view. It discusses punishment, order, and justice, and it shows teachers ways to approach the more serious problems attached to maintaining good discipline in the classroom, as well as ways of helping students arrive at self-discipline.

231. The Disruptive Student and the Teacher. NEA Professional Studies Series. Rivers, L. Wendell, ERIC Clearinghouse on Teacher Education, Washington, DC, 1977, 42p (ED 144 931; Reprint: EDRS-HC not available; also available from National Education Association, 1201 Sixteenth St., N.W., Washington, DC 20036).

Methods are described for the classroom management of disruptive children, defined as those who cannot be classified as emotionally disturbed or mentally retarded but who, either periodically or chronically, cause problems in classroom management or discipline. No attempt is made to provide exhaustive theoretical background, but rather concentration upon practical suggestions that can be used by the teacher in managing disruptive behavior. Theory that is discussed is based upon the premise that disruptive behavior is a form of communicative behavior—i.e., the basis for most disruptive behavior is a state of pupil distress manifested by the child as a result of conditions prevailing in the home, at school, or both. Each chapter is divided into three parts, discussing (1) background information concerning the topic under investigation, (2) objectives relating to the role of the teacher in management of disruptive behavior, and (3) recommended techniques for the management of such behavior. Topics discussed are: (1) the nature of disruptive behavior; (2) the disruptive child; (3) general management techniques; (4) the disruptive classroom; (5) when to call for help; (6) the emotionally disrupted child; (7) the disrupted teacher; and (8) research findings relating to disruptive behavior in the classroom.

232. The L.E.A.S.T. Approach to Classroom Discipline. Description of Teacher Inservice Education materials. National Education Association, Washington, DC, Project on Utilization of Inservice Education R & D Outcomes, Jul 1978, 8p. Sponsoring agency: National Institute of Education (DHEW), Washington, DC (ED 166 143; Reprint: EDRS).

The inservice teacher education program described here focuses on a system of employing minimum action in order to attain and maintain effective classroom discipline, and offers a survival strategy for the classroom teacher. The product title is an acronym for the five steps or options outlined for achieving classroom discipline: (1) leave things alone because no problems are likely to occur; (2) end the action indirectly because behavior is disrupting the classroom; (3) attend more fully because more information or communication is needed; (4) spell out directions because disruption or harm will occur; and (5) track student progress to evaluate and reinforce student behavior. Information is provided concerning program purposes, content, activities, resources, and history of development. A critique and ordering information are also included.

233. Management of Disruptive Surface Behavior: Prescriptive Learning Package 5. Description of Teacher Inservice Education Mateials. National Education Association, Washington, DC, Apr 1977, 8p; Research provided by NEA Project on Utilization of Inservice Education R&D Outcomes. Sponsoring agency: National Institute of Education (DHEW), Washington, DC (ED 164 536; Reprint: EDRS).

A prescriptive learning package for inservice teacher education is described. The package seeks to aid the teacher in developing and implementing individualized intervention techniques suitable for children whose learning situations result in disruptive behavior; knowledge and applications of terms and principles of behavior management are highlighted. Information is provided on the purposes and content of the package, activities and resources necessary for implementation, history of development, and ordering information. A critique is also provided.

234. Managing Inappropriate Behaviors in the Classroom. Lovitt, Thomas C., Council for Exceptional Children, Reston, VA, Information Center on Exceptional Children, 1978, 54p. Sponsoring agency: National Institute of Education (DHEW), Washington, DC (ED 157 255; Reprint: EDRS; also available from Council for Exceptional Children, Publication Sales Unit, 1920 Association Drive, Reston, VA 22091).

The booklet provides information on a number of strategies for teachers to use in managing disruptive behaviors in the classroom. On the first section several approaches (such as token economies) are discussed that pertain to the general, comprehensive management of classes. Included in Section II are several strategies (including taking away something to attenuate behavior) that may be used with individuals who display inappropriate behaviors. A final section contains information on three approaches to group management: individual consequences contingent on individuals, group consequence contingent on individuals, and group consequence contingent on the group. A final section offers six considerations (such as defining principles by function and reviewing a variety of techniques) in the management of disruptive behaviors.

235. Managing the Preschool Classroom (Preschool—Third Grade). Brown, Judy, Far West Laboratory for Educational Research and Development, San Francisco, CA, 1975, 85p. Sponsoring agency: National Institute of Education (DHEW), Washington, DC (ED 129 453; Reprint: EDRS; also available from Far West Laboratory for Educational Research and Development, 1855 Folsom Street, San Francisco, CA 94103).

This unit of the Flexible Learning System (FLS) provides training on how to use classroom planning to avoid management problems and techniques to reduce inappropriate behavior in the classroom. Management is approached as the process of organizing and structuring the classroom, its activities, and the responsibilities of staff and children. Management is directed toward helping children assume responsibility for their own behavior in a climate designed to maximize individual freedom and minimize disturbances in the learning environment. Criteria for classroom management establishing rules and limits, scheduling, and the provisioning and use of materials are explored in the context of minimizing the occurrence of management problems. Practice is provided in developing rules and limits, arranging classroom activities, developing daily plans, demonstrating the arrangement of materials, and extending and adapting classroom materials to meet individual needs. In a discussion on how to handle inappropriate behavior, topics include: determining the problem; anticipating and redirecting inappropriate behavior; attending to positive behavior, contingent use of classroom activities, using time out, and why punishment is an inappropriate form of classroom management. Activities involve classroom observation, demonstration, working with children, thought, and problem-solving activities.

236. A Manual on Nonviolence and Children.
Judson, Stephanie, Comp., Friends Peace Committee, Philadelphia, PA, 1977, 158p. (ED 167 242; Reprint: EDRS; also available from Nonviolence and Children Program, Friends Peace Committee, 1515 Cherry Street, Philadelphia, PA 19102).

This manual on teaching children nonviolent attitudes and the skills for nonviolent conflict resolution suggests teaching activities and methods, describes classrooms in which these methods have been employed, and explains the underlying theory of conflict resolution. The first part of the manual, an outgrowth of the Friends' Nonviolence and Children Program, presents the theory (based on reevaluation counseling) and suggests teaching methods in terms of (1) the affirmation of self and others, (2) sharing information and experiences, (3) conflict resolution, and (4) problem-solving approaches. The second part gives actual examples and personal accounts of how the theory has been used in several schools and discusses additional procedures for creating a nonviolent atmosphere: meeting facilitation, staffings, and parent support groups. The manual concludes with a bibliography of appropriate children's books and descriptions of cooperative games are included.

237. Professional Teacher Education Module Series. Assist Students in Developing Self-Discipline, Module E-7 of Category E—Instructional Management.
Ohio State University, Columbus, National Center for Research in Vocational Education, 1977, 39p. Sponsoring agency: National Institute of Education (DHEW), Washington, DC (ED 149 106; Reprint: EDRS; also available from: American Association for Vocational Instructional Materials (AAVIM), 120 Engineering Center, University of Georgia, Athens, GA 30602).

This seventh in a series of nine learning modules on instructional management is designed to assist secondary and postsecondary vocational teachers in identifying and using classroom procedures to develop self-discipline in students, and in developing the type of environment which allows learning to take place. The terminal objective for the module is to assist students in developing self-discipline in an actual school situation. Introductory sections relate the competency dealt with in this module to others in the program and list both the enabling objectives for the four learning exeriences and the resources required. Materials in the learning experiences include required reading, a self-check quiz and a model

answer, class rules, a rules guidelines checklist, case studies, model critiques, and the teacher performance assessment form for use in evaluation of the terminal objective. (The modules on instructional management are part of a larger series of 100 field-tested performance-based teacher education (PBTE) self-contained learning packages for use in preservice or inservice training of teachers in all occupational areas. Materials are designed for use by teachers, either on an individual or group basis, working under the direction of one or more resource persons/instructors.)

238. Project TEACH (Teacher Effectiveness and Classroom Handling). Description of Teacher Inservice Education Materials.
National Education Association, Washington, DC, Project on Utilization of Inservice Education R & D Outcomes, Jan 1978, 8p. Sponsoring agency: National Institute of Education (DHEW), Washington, DC (ED 167 527; Reprint: EDRS).

The teacher program described here focuses on options for dealing positively with the day-to-day problems and occurrences in the classroom and reducing psychic and physical drain on the teacher. Emphasis is on positive management and relational skills, i.e., verbal skills, momentum building, and nonconfrontation strategies, and decision-making techniques. Information is provided here on the purposes and content of the program and materials, as well as activities and resources involved. A critique, history of development, and ordering information are also included.

239. Strategies for Handling the Disruptive Student.
Levitt, Linda Karen; Rutherford, Robert B., Arizona Educational Information System, Arizona State University, Tempe, AZ, 1978, 105p.

This resource guide contains suggestions for educators on how to: (1) identify the disruptive student and disruptive behavior, (2) develop strategies which will avert disruptive behavior before it occurs, and (3) develop strategies for dealing with and eliminating disruptive behaviors once they do occur. Included are screening and recording tests, models for changing behavior, plus an extensive bibliography.

BOOKS

240. The Acting-Out Child: Coping with Classroom Disruption.
Walker, Hill M. Boston: Allyn and Bacon, Inc., 1979, 312p.

This book provides practical guidelines and techniques for channeling student energy towards constructive learning rather than disruptive behavior. Each technique is divided into five sections: definition, examples, guidelines for correct application, issues to consider, and advantages and disadvantages. Included are charts and diagrams for establishing record keeping procedures and interpreting test results, detailed case studies providing first hand examples, mastery questions to test the reader's comprehension, and extensive references for further reading.

241. Alternative Teaching Strategies: Helping Behaviorally Troubled Children Achieve. A Guide for Teachers and Psychologists. Swift, Marshall S.; Spivack, George. Champaign, IL: Research Press, 1975, 217p.

This book provides (1) specific information about overt classroom behaviors that affect or reflect academic success or failure, and (2) information and suggestions about alternative teaching strategies that may be used to increase behavioral effectiveness and subsequent academic achievement. The focus of the book is on specific behaviors, behavior groupings, and total behavior patterns of children which, through a long series of research projects, have been shown to describe and distinguish successful and unsuccessful students throughout the elementary school grades. This focus is coupled with extensive step-by step descriptions of alternative teaching strategies that can be practically incorporated into plans for each child or groups of children in the classroom. The first chapter, concerning the proportion of children displaying disturbance in school, provides the teacher, and those with responsibility to help the teacher, with a realistic picture of how many children are having difficulty coping in the classroom. Each of the next ten chapters provides extensive and detailed descriptions of specific, feasible teaching alternatives for working with students displaying each of the achievement-related behavior dimensions mentioned in Chapter 1. The focus of the last chapter is upon common elements among teaching strategies. In this chapter previous discussions of alternative teaching strategies are reviewed.

242. Behavior Modification: A Practical Guide for the Classroom Teacher. Howie, Patricia Anzalone. West Nyack, NY: Parker Publishing Company, Inc., 1977, 214p.

This book describes applications of behavior modification and is a blueprint for evaluating and imroving the behavioral characteristics of the individual child. Explains how to identify and analyze the causes behind the behavioral problems observed in students and presents techniques for modifying abnormal behavioral responses. Discusses the arrangement of the classroom and how it affects the response of your students; how to use rewards and reinforcers properly; how to handle the special needs of the disruptive child; how to help children with an attitude of defeat; how to get the quiet, unresponsive child to participate; and step-by-step guidance in modifying behavior. Case studies demonstrate the handling of many types of problems.

243. Classroom Discipline for Effective Teaching and Learning. Tanner, Laurel N. New York: Holt, Rinehart and Winston, 1978, 214p.

The intent of this book is to present the developmental stages of discipline and a conceptual framework for the role of the teachers. Chapters cover the nature of discipline, discipline and development, discipline and the curriculum, teaching (including teacher authority), lack of attention and teacher expectation, discipline in special settings (such as open classrooms), the ecology of classroom discipline, socialization, discipline problems, and the needs and rights of students. The author maintains that it is important for short-range disciplinary measures to be consonant with long-range developmental goals.

244. Classroom Management and Teaching: Persistent Problems and Rational Solutions. Epstein, Charlotte. Reston, VA: Reston Publishing, 1979, 302p.

Good classroom management is basic to good teaching, but when one or more children demonstrate problem behavior then discipline must rank high on the list of priorities. The book suggests the application of behavioral modification theory to a varied selection of classroom problems and suggests practical, workable approaches to resolving difficult situations. The methods deal with a fundamental analysis of the environmental and personality variables that can form a breeding ground for disciplinary and learning problems. Talking out of turn, physical roughness, refusal to complete lessons, and similar behaviors can turn a classroom into a virtual prison for teacher and children alike. Conversely, when the causes of these behaviors are carefully examined, behavioral modification can provide humane, effective, and extremely efficient solutions that make the classroom a much more pleasant place.

245. Discipline: A Shared Experience. Welch, Ira David; Hughes, Wanda. New York: Hart Publishing Co., 1977, 217p.

Using examples of specific discipline problems that occur with preteenagers at school and at home, such as graffiti, rudeness, foul language, teasing, and tattling; the authors outline a discipline philosophy in which children learn responsibility and self-control from adults, who act not as total authority figures, but as experienced guides and exemplars of good behavior.

246. Discipline and Classroom Management. Osborn, D. Keith; Osborn, Janie Dyson. Athens, GA: Educational Associates, 1977, 108p.

The authors offer practical classroom management techniques based on reinforcement, modeling, and influence theories, as well as their own theory of discipline. Series of questions lead the reader through self-analysis of his/her own teaching behaviors and through case study observation and analysis of student behavior problem areas, such as cultural differences, physical/learning problems, and interpersonal difficulties. Learning objectives are included for each chapter of this text.

247. Discipline and the Classroom Teacher. Faust, Naomi F. Port Washington, NY: Kennikat Press, 1977, 203p.

A number-one concern of teachers throughout the nation is "disciplinary problems." The purpose of this book is to assist teachers in acquiring the feeling of being able to establish well-disciplined classes in which adequate learning may take place. Several chapters are devoted to handling disadvantaged youth in discipline and learning. Much of the book, however, is concerned with the discipline of all types of youngsters. The book puts great emphasis on using preventive measures for problems in discipline, but suggests ways of handling disciplinary problems when they occur.

248. Discipline in the Junior High/Middle School: A Handbook for Teachers, Counselors, and Administrators. Stradley, William E; Aspinall, Richard D. New York: The Center for Applied Research in Education, Inc., 1975, 227p.

This book gives middle-level teachers methods and techniques for solving the student behavior problems that they face when working with early adolescents. The ideas presented were selected on the basis of practicality, adaptability to differing teacher needs, and relationship to the special needs of early adolescents. The "how to" sections include: using preventive discipline, helping students improve their self-images, developing respect for authority, improving student-peer relationships, resolving student-teacher conflicts, reducing attendance problems, and reducing vandalism.

249. Discipline in the Schools: A Guide to Reducing Misbehavior. Deitz, Samuel M.; Hummel, John H. Englewood Cliffs, NJ: Educational Technology Publications, 1978, 279p.

The main purpose of this book is to present and explain a large variety of procedures from which a teacher may choose when faced with problems of misbehavior. While mostly oriented toward solving problems with elementary and middle-school-aged children, the solutions presented also work with young adults. The book is divided into three sections. Section I deals with issues in identifying, defining, and measuring misbehaviors and also with evaluating programs for their reduction. Section II discusses ten procedures which have been found to be effective for reducing or eliminating misbehavior. The first four either use aversive events or produce some form of aversive behavioral side effects. The last six procedures reduce misbehavior through more positive or productive teacher-student interactions. Section III is a summary. Within each section, the book is divided into a number of units, each presenting a complete discussion of one or more specific skills necessary for the effective reduction of misbehavior. Each unit begins with a list of study questions and ends with a list of suggested projects.

250. Effective Classroom Management. Wallen, Carl J.; Wallen, LaDonna L. Boston: Allyn and Bacon, Inc., 1978, 340p.

This book is divided into three sections, one for each of the teacher's major roles—instructional manager, group leader, and counselor. Each section includes theories, conditions, strategies, and assessment techniques necessary for carrying out each of the roles.

251. Helping Students Help Themselves. How You Can Put Behavior Analysis into Action in Your Classroom. Goodwin, Dwight L.; Coates, Thomas J. Englewood Cliffs, NJ: Prentice-Hall, Inc., 1976, 205p.

Chapters 1 and 2 of this book introduce basic concepts and assumptions in behavior analysis and are especially important for the inexperienced teacher, since they lay the groundwork for what is to come. Chapters 3 through 9 provide detailed steps to be followed in using behavior analysis to improve the learning and behavior of students. This is the heart of the book for all teachers. The last chapters show applications of behavior analysis that have been developed within the past few years—strategies for groups of students or for the entire class; teaching personal effectiveness skills; and ways to teach students how to manage and control their own behavior.

252. Inservice Teacher Training Materials: Individualizing Instruction, Classroom Management/Discipline, Motivation. New York: EPIE Institute, 1977, 130p.

This report contains detailed descriptions of 49 sets of materials designed to be used for inservice teacher training in individualizing instruction, classroom management and discipline, and motivation. The report attempts to provide consumer information for teachers choosing materials for inservice training. Each entry consists of a summary of the materials as well as a detailed description. The summary includes the following information: title, publication date, intended users, grade levels, number of participants, primary focus, school subjects or inservice topics covered, activities and resources involved in using the materials, price range, and a describer critique. The detailed description includes additional information on purpose, content, activities and resources, evaluation of teacher inservice learning, ordering information, history of development, and describer and user critiques. Most materials listed are intended for teachers in elementary and/or secondary grades.

253. The Last Straw: A Handbook of Solutions to School Behavior Problems. Volkmann, Christina S. Palo Alto, CA: R & E Research Associates, Inc., 1978, 105p.

This informally written handbook for elementary school teachers describes typical classroom behavioral problems and proposes ways of dealing with them. The "problem" student is identified as one who requires the teacher's personal energy or reactions, drawing attention away from the remainder of the class and creating added burdens for the teacher. Nineteen specific categories of problem students are described, including the bully, the quiet one, the superior snob, and the sneak. For each category, possible solutions to the behavior problem are described. Penalties that students may be subjected to in case the solutions prove to be inadequate are also suggested. In addition, general suggestions pertaining to ways of building a classroom behavioral foundation are discussed. These include daily, informal conversation sessions which allow for free discourse between teacher and students, parental involvement, and careful attention to the physical arrangement of the classroom.

254. Maintaining Discipline in Classroom Instruction. Gnagey, William J. New York: Macmillan, 1975, 50p.

This document focuses on classroom discipline and how the teacher can maintain an environment that will optimize appropriate learning. Part 1 defines classroom discipline. Part 2 discusses classroom misbehavior and describes a number of classroom management techniques. Part 3 offers suggestions for control techniques. Part 4 discusses techniques for gaining control over an entire class by successfully disciplining one of its leaders. Part 5 presents behavior modification using five principles of behavior change. Part 6 looks at abrasive and deprivative punishment and its side effects on the learning process. Part 7 compares the use of reward and punishment as disciplinary measures in the classroom. Part 8 presents a description of William Glasser's therapeutic approach to classroom discipline. The appendixes include an evaluation device for the classroom teacher and a bibliography.

255. Making It Till Friday: A Guide to Successful Classroom Management. Long, James D.; Frye, Virginia H. Princeton, NJ: Princeton Book Company, 1977, 200p.

The purpose of this book is to provide teachers and prospective teachers at all grade levels with practical suggestions, based on the research literature, for managing their classrooms more effectively. Chapters cover: the meaning of classroom management; the interaction of attitudes and behavior; setting the stage for desirable behavior; accenting the positive; managing disruptive behavior; working with resource staff and parents; guiding students toward self-management; and ethical and legal problems in classroom management.

School-Level Discipline: Advice to Administrators

Legal Issues/Due Process

JOURNAL ARTICLES

256. **Administrative Prerogative: Restraints of Natural Justice on Student Discipline.** Alexander, Kern. *Journal of Law and Education*. v7, n3, p331–58, Jul 1978 (EJ 183 307; Reprint: UMI).

Examines how the British concept of natural justice and the American concept of due process have produced legal precedents that place new and extra-statutory requirements on administrative disciplinary actions that administrators must accommodate if students are to be given maximum legal fairness and equity.

257. **Due Process in Discipline.** Alberti, Charles E. *Clearing House*. v51, n1, p12–14, Sep 1977 (EJ 169 086; Reprint: UMI).

The enjoyment of the right of attending school is conditioned necessarily on compliance by pupils with the reasonable rules, regulations, and requirements of the school authorities. Discusses the legal decisions that set the foundation for developing school discipline and responsibilities of administrators, educators, as well as school districts in maintaining discipline policy.

258. **Hard Choices in School Discipline and Hardening of Due Process Mold.** Kola, A. A. *Journal of Law and Education*. v4, n4, p583–86, Oct 1975.

Stated is the belief that the case of Goss v Lopez, long hailed as a landmark victory for student rights, was decided as it was because the Supreme Court majority wanted to humanize relationships between students and school authorities, but actually may have achieved just the opposite result by curbing the discretion of school authorities and hardening the due process mold.

259. **In Perspective: School Violence and Discipline.** Mallory, Arthur L. *School Business Affairs*. v43, n7, p155–56, Jul 1977.

Due process requirements should not be an excuse for failing to maintain firm standards of conduct. Due process demands that policies for discipline and punishment be established, and these policies will help by spelling out the rights and options of both students and educators.

260. **In-School Punishment for Out-of-School Offenses.** Hobbs, Gardner J. *GAMSP Journal*. v1, n2, p54–59, Fall 1977 (ED 151 925; Reprint: EDRS).

This paper examines the reported decisions, one unreported decision, and two attorney generals' opinions that deal with school punishment for the use of drugs and alcohol off campus and with suspensions pending criminal charges for student offenses committed off school property.

261. **Liability in Student Discipline Cases.** Reutter, E. Edmund, Jr. *IAR Research Bulletin*. v15, n4, p1, 8–9, May 1975.

Discusses the U.S. Supreme Court's 1975 ruling that school officials are liable to civil suits when they violate a student's constitutional rights through "ignorance or disregard of settled, indisputable law." After examining implications of the decision, the author concludes that no unjustified burdens have been imposed on school officials.

262. **The Nuts and Bolts of Procedural Due Process.** MacFeeley, Richard W. *Phi Delta Kappan*. v57, n1, p26, Sep 1975.

An urban school district's model for procedural due process designed to meet the requirements of the Goss decision.

263. **Student Wrongs versus Student Rights.** *Nation's Schools and Colleges*. v2, n4, p31–38, Apr 1975.

Recent Supreme Court decisions and reports from student advocacy groups clash with the realities of the classroom and put administrators in a quandary.

264. The Supreme Court and the Daily Life of Schools: Implications of Goss v. Lopez. Weckstein, Paul. *Inequality in Education.* v20, p47–57, Jul 1975.

Examines two important questions about the implications of the Goss and Wood decisions—what is the general picture of education that emerges in these decisions, and to what extent is the due process model applicable to school decisions other than suspension and expulsion?

265. Verbal Chastisement in Elementary and Secondary Schools: A Suggestion. Stevens, George E. *Journal of Law and Education.* v6, n3, p319–25, Jul 1977 (EJ 165 822; Reprint: UMI).

Discusses educators' potential liability for verbal chastisement of students in elementary and secondary schools and suggests a legal standard that might be applied to such behavior.

266. Young People and the Law: The Dilemma. Schmit, Marilyn C. *School Business Affairs.* v43, n6, p132, Jun 1977 (EJ 164 186; Reprint: UMI).

Excessive emphasis on the rights of the youthful offender without sufficient acknowledgment of his/her corresponding responsibility is not always in the best interest of the individual.

REPORTS

267. An Administrator's Legal Guide to Student Control. Connors, Eugene T., James Madison University, Harrisonburg, VA, 1978, 136p; not available in paper copy due to broken print in original document (ED 170 923; Reprint: EDRS).

The purpose of this study was to help public school administrators, especially principals, to understand the legal and constitutional limitations of their authority in dealing with students. Control of students is discussed as five separate topics, each representing a chapter, as follows: (1) freedom of expression and First Amendment rights; (2) the constitutionality of dress and hair style codes; (3) due process and suspension and expulsion; (4) the constitutionality of searches and seizures; and (5) the rights of the married or pregnant student. Two student rights cases—Tinker v Des Moines Independent Community School District and Goss v Lopez—are discussed in detail. The study concludes that public school administrators must respect the civil rights of all students as specified in the Constitution.

268. An Analysis of Students' Rights and School Discipline.* Rowles, Terry Lee, Arizona State University, 1978, 242p (78–15,241; Reprint: DC).

It was the problem of this investigation to delineate the most fundamental of students' rights in the state of Arizona in the areas of freedom of expression, personal appearance, corporal punishment, and due process of law; to generally discuss these rights as they pertain to school discipline; and to outline the recent trends in the field of school law concerning students' rights.

Forty-four court decisions were presented which the investigator found to be most relevant to the topic of students' rights and school discipline as they pertain to freedom of expression, personal appearance, corporal punishment, and due process of law.

The cases summarized here include those which have been decided in state, district, circuit, and U.S. Supreme courts and may apply either specifically to Arizona or to other jurisdictions. Each case summary indicates (1) the issue(s) involved, (2) the background of the case, (3) the decision, and, if applicable, (4) the significance and/or consequences of the decision as determined by the researcher.

Some of the conclusions and recommendations made by the author were as follows:

1. The fundamental students' rights in the area of freedom of expression, personal appearance, corporal punishment, and due process of law are generally those which are guaranteed to all citizens in the first ten amendments to the United States Constitution.

2. School officials may not establish and enforce rules and regulations which are arbitrary, capricious, or unreasonable.

3. Students' constitutional rights may not be limited without due process of law.

4. Students may legally be punished for those behaviors or actions which result in the infringement of the rights of others or in the interference with the mission of the school.

5. School officials should be familiar with local regulations and school board policies which govern discipline in their schools.

6. Educators should be aware of the most fundamental of recent court decisions involving students' rights.

7. Educators should make an honest and sincere attempt to understand the rationale of the recent court decisions which have extended to students the rights which are guaranteed to all citizens in the United States Constitution.

8. School officials should endeavor to protect the rights of all students by making and enforcing rules which are fair and reasonable and directly related to the work of the school in providing a free public education to all students.

269. The Courts and Student Conduct. ERIC/CEM State-of-the-Knowledge-Series, Number Twenty-seven, NOLPE Monograph Series. Reutter, E. Edmund, Jr., National Organization on Legal Problems of Education, Topeka, KS; Oregon University, Eugene, ERIC Clearinghouse on Educational Management, 1975, 104p. Sponsoring agency: National Institute of Education (DHEW), Washington, DC (ED 102 641; Reprint: EDRS; also available from National Organization on Legal Problems in Education, 825 Western Avenue, Topeka, KS).

This monograph analyzes and summarizes judicial decisions relevant to the control of student conduct by school officials. It is an expansion and revision of a monograph published by the same author in 1970. Extensive revision of the earlier work was necessary because the number of appellate court decisions involving student conduct has grown rapidly in recent years as a result of increased reliance on the courts as the means to resolve conflicts between students and school authorities. The author first describes the general legal framework that applies to student discipline and then examines court decisions relevant to various specific areas of student conduct, including dress and appearance, insignias and emblems, publications, secret societies, and marriage and parenthood.

270. Discipline, Corporal Punishment, and Suspension. Smith, Raymond C. Apr 1975, 16p; Paper presented at the Annual Meeting of the National School Boards Association (35th, Miami Beach, FL, April 1975); not available in hard copy due to marginal legibility of original document (ED 106 920; Reprint: EDRS).

During the past decade, and especially since 1970, there have been great changes in the manner in which students are disciplined. The greatest single influence has not been the effort of enlightened educators or crusading boards of education, but rather change has taken place mainly as a result of decrees from our judicial system. A review of court litigation reveals that a student does not give up any of his rights when he enters the schoolhouse; that students are entitled to be heard and to receive due process; that when a student's rights are being protected, the school need not be afraid to act; and that continued judicial impact on education should be expected. The best way to minimize the role of the courts in education is to eliminate violations of law and individual rights. This can be done by reviewing district policies and practices and by training administrators to use procedures that are both legally acceptable and administratively effective. As helpful as these administrative steps are, nothing helps avoid discipline problems as much as a good instructional program—especially one that is effective in helping those students who are furthest behind in reading and math.

271. Due Process Workshop Packet: Sample Forms, Procedures, and Correspondence. Orange County Department of Education, Santa Ana, CA, 15p.

This Due Process Workshop Packet contains sample forms, procedures, and correspondence for the following areas: Due Process High School Discipline Report, Anecdotal Record, Teacher Comments, Sample Notices of Suspension Sent to Parents from an Elementary Principal and from a High School Principal, Extension of Suspension Notice, Expulsion Request Referral, Expulsion Hearing Notice, Procedures for Expulsion Hearing Panel, and Due Process Index.

272. Hair and Dress Code: Update. A Legal Memorandum. Gluckman, Ivan, National Association of Secondary School Principals, Reston, VA, Jan 1976, 76p. (ED 116 343; Reprint: EDRS— HC not available; also available from National Association of Secondary School Principals, 1904 Association Drive, Reston, VA 22091).

School regulations concerning hair have been successfully defended in appellate courts in about half the country. The most recent decision of a federal circuit court upholding a school's rules was decided in 1975. In this instance the court reversed the position it held only three years earlier. There are some guidelines that should be kept in mind if a school has hair regulations or is considering their adoption: rules should be drawn as narrowly and specifically as possible and should be clearly related to the educational purposes of the school; the strongest legal bases for hair and grooming regulations are the protection of health, safety, or educational performance of the students; if the rule is based on the need to prevent disruption of the educational process, the school should be prepared to meet the test outlined in the Tinker decision; it should be made sure that the rule is not grounded solely on sexual stereotypes or other presuppositions that cannot be defended against charges of sex discrimination; and the rule should be spelled out, preferably in writing, and made known to everyone it will affect, before it is enforced against anyone.

273. The Law of Procedure in Student Suspensions and Expulsions. Phay, Robert E., National Organization on Legal Problems of Education, Topeka, KS: Oregon University, Eugene, ERIC Clearinghouse on Educational Management, Sep 1977, 64p; not available in paper copy due to small print size of much of the document. Sponsoring agency: National Institute of Education (DHEW), Washington, DC (ED 146 661; Reprint: EDRS; also available from National Organization on Legal Problems of Education, 5401 Southwest 7th Avenue, Topeka, KS 66606).

This state-of-the-knowledge paper, a companion to the author's 1975 monograph on a similar topic, examines the legal ramifications of student suspension, expulsion, and search and seizure of students' property. The author reviews relevant court litigation and state laws pertaining to specific rules on student conduct, the procedures to follow in suspension and expulsion cases (including the hearing, the student's right to counsel, inspection of evidence, impartiality of the hearing, witnesses, self-incrimination, mass hearings, hearing transcripts, appeal, and automatic review), and multiple and short-term suspensions, as well as the law relating to search and seizure. He concludes that, although many may consider procedural due process requirements to constitute serious interference with internal school discipline, constitutional standards require only that students be treated fairly and granted the type of due process that school administrators would demand for themselves.

274. Methods of Discipline: What Is Allowed? A Legal Memorandum. Nolte, M. Chester, National Association of Secondary School Principals, Reston, VA, 1976, 7p (ED 123 709; Reprint: EDRS—HC not available; also available from National Association of Secondary School Principals, 1904 Association Drive, Reston, VA 22091).

This publication briefly discusses the legal status of various methods of school discipline and related efforts to control the behavior of elementary and secondary school students. Specific topics examined include corporal punishment, suspension, expulsion, exclusion from extracurricular activities, detention, truancy, verbal correction, a variety of less common disciplinary measures, and the relationship of school discipline and the responsibility of school officials to civil justice. Usually the discussion of these topics consists mainly of brief quotations taken directly from court opinions in relevant cases.

275. The Reasonable Exercise of Authority, II. Ackerly, Robert L.; Gluckman, Ivan B., National Association of Secondary School Principals, Reston, VA, 1976, 40p (ED 117 845; Reprint: EDRS—HC not available; also available from National Association of Secondary School Principals, 1904 Association Drive, Reston, VA 22091).

This document was prepared in order to provide principals and other administrators with information and guidance on their duties and powers as determined by constitutional and statutory interpretation in the hopes that such information will help them stay out of the courts. More specifically, the document considers the basic and general legal principles of due process and suggests acceptable approaches to the necessary and reasonable exercise of authority by school officials. After a lengthy discussion of due process, a number of related topics are discussed individually. The topics are freedom of expression, student publications, personal appearance, religion and patriotism, civil rights, codes of behavior, student property, weapons and drugs, extracurricular activities, discipline, corporal punishment, student participation in school governance, the right to petition, and student records.

276. Student Rights and Discipline. Schofield, Dee; Dunn, Pierre. Association of California School Administrators; Oregon University, Eugene, ERIC Clearinghouse on Educational Management, 1977, 33p. Sponsoring agency: National Institute of Education (DHEW), Washington, DC (ED 137 897; Reprint: EDRS; also available from Association of California School Administrators, P.O. Box 39186, Rincon Annex, San Francisco).

The conflict between authoritarianism and democracy is almost nowhere more obvious than in the controversial area of student rights. In loco parentis, long an integral part of educational practice, is no longer an accepted role for educators to assume toward students. Directly counter to in loco parentis is the concept of due process of law for students. This review of the literature examines the key court decisions establishing such civil liberties for students as First Amendment rights, freedom from unreasonable search and seizure, the right of students to examine their records, equal treatment for handicapped students, and freedom from discrimination on the basis of race or sex. In regard to student rights, the school administrator's position is not an enviable one. The ambiguity surrounding the student rights controversy makes hard and fast answers difficult to come by. But the schools can become the setting for achieving balance between the opposing forces evident in both the student rights controversy and in the society as a whole.

277. Student Rights and Responsibilities Revisited: Current Trends in School Policies and Programs. Graul, Donald; Jones, J. William, National School Public Relations Association, Arlington, VA, 1976, 66p (ED 122 441; Reprint: EDRS—HC not available; also available from National School Public Relations Association, 1801 North Moore Street, Arlington, VA 22209, Stock No. 411-13325).

Because recent legislation and court decisions have expanded the rights of all students, schools of the seventies must educate them about the responsibilities that go with these newly recognized rights. A nationwide survey indicates that many schools have established grievance procedures based on open communication and clearly stated policies. And many have taken steps to ensure due process in suspension and expulsion and to safeguard confidentiality of student records. The report looks at the old issues of student government, the student press, and student discipline. The implications of Title IX and the legal responsibility of school board members for ensuring student rights are described. Useful as a handbook of dissemination techniques, the report is illustrated with samples from the content and graphics of student rights codes.

278. **Student Suspension and Expulsion Procedures: A Model Policy and Rules, with Comments, for Assistance to Local Boards in Meeting the Requirements of Procedural Due Process in Dealing with Student Suspension and Expulsion.** Iowa State Department of Public Instruction, Des Moines, IA, May 1975, 21p (ED 120 907; Reprint: EDRS).

With their emphasis on due process, these model rules and policies can help schools safeguard the rights of students and ensure that schools are more certain of the facts when all other alternatives have failed and it is necessary to dismiss or expel a student. Local rules and policies based on this model should help to keep both the rights and responsibilities of the student and the school in perspective.

Philosophy, Guidelines, Model Policies

JOURNAL ARTICLES

279. **Behavioral Analysis: The Principal and Discipline.** Boyd, John D.; Bowers, Rolland A. *Clearing House.* v48, n7, p420–26, Mar 1974.

The purpose of this article is not to present a panacea nor to argue for either the hickory stick or permissiveness. Instead, a more reasoned compromise based on some of the psychological principles that govern the development of responsible social behavior is recommended.

280. **Bit of Philosophy, Lot of Experience in Discipline.** Rodgers, Duane O. *Thrust for Educational Leadership.* v8, n4, p32,29, Mar 1979.

Written in the form of a memo from a principal to his vice principal, 15 points are offered to aid in reducing discipline problems in a high school.

281. **The Chronic Disciplinary Problem.** Garrett, George. *Catalyst for Change.* v7, n1, p6–9, Feb 1977 (EJ 169 706; Reprint: UMI).

Discusses some of the ways students' behavior problems may be related to their peer group, home life, or physical problems, and offers guidelines for school administrators to follow in dealing with chronic disciplinary problem pupils.

282. **The Counselor and Student Discipline: Suggested Roles.** Bickel, Frank; O'Neill, Maude. *Personnel and Guidance Journal.* v57, n10, p522–25, Jun 1979 (EJ 202 831; Reprint: UMI).

Provides summary and analysis of literature on the counselor's role in school discipline. Roles are grouped into six categories: mediator, ombudsman, consultant, psychological educator, special program developer, and counselor. Counselors may find roles that satisfy the needs of their students and are appropriate to their own personalities and skill levels.

283. **Discipline: An Inalienable Right of Both Schools and Students.** Stenson, Victor J. *Journal of the International Association of Pupil Personnel Workers.* v23, n3, p158, 163–68, Jun 1979 (EJ 202 858; Reprint: UMI).

School-parent-student negotiations are plans in which the school can utilize negative reinforcers along with positive reinforcers. For schools to operate at optimum level, the method used to treat student problems must be balanced between negative and positive modes of treatment.

284. **Discretion in School Discipline.** Manley-Casimir, Michael E. *Interchange.* v8, n1–2, p84–100, 1977–78 (EJ 176 436; Reprint: UMI).

It is in cases where disruptive students are dealt with by school disciplinarians possessing extensive discretionary power that the school's recognition or denial of student rights and interest assumes sharpest focus.

285. **Disorders in Our Schools: Causes and Remedies.** Glasser, William. *Phi Delta Kappan.* v59, n5, p331–33, Jan 1978 (EJ 169 846; Reprint: UMI).

The answer to better discipline is giving students a stake in the school, caring for them, and teaching them without failure.

286. From Discipline to Responsibility Training: A Humanistic Orientation for the School. Bratter, Thomas Edward. *Psychology in the Schools.* v14, n1, p45–53, Jan 1977.

A nine-step discipline process, which can become a profound learning experience for potentially disruptive students, provides numerous opportunities to become more responsible and to adopt more productive behavior for those who move through the system.

287. A Hard-Nosed Principal's Hard-Nosed Advice on School Discipline. *American School Board Journal.* v165, n4, p32–34, 56, Apr 1978 (EJ 175 688; Reprint: UMI).

The school's must create a climate of reason and respect, and prevent negative self-images, humiliation, and failure. Perhaps 80 percent of the discipline problems in schools involve things the schools can affect.

288. The Hard Rules for Enforcing Discipline in Your Schools. *American School Board Journal.* v165, n3, p29–32,63, Mar 1978 (EJ 173 617; Reprint: UMI).

Presents tough-minded advice on how school leaders can maintain discipline while minimizing the possibility that they will trample student rights or face court charges. Such areas as search and seizure, dress codes, and due process are covered.

289. In-School Truancy in Urban Schools—Problem and a Solution. Teachman, G. W. *Phi Delta Kappan.* v61, n3, p203–05, Nov 1979.

Teachers report that nearly 30 percent of the students in Detroit high schools will be absent from each class on an average day, disrupting or destroying effective instruction. Here is hard-nosed advice on corrective measures.

290. A Model of School Discipline. Tanner, Laurel N. *Teachers College Record.* v80, n4, p734–42, May 1979 (EJ 203 940; Reprint: UMI).

The model presented is intended to return discipline to a legitimate place in education and educational research; it focuses on three elements—pupil development, ecological factors, and disciplinary approaches.

291. *NAASP Bulletin.* v63, n428, Sep 1979.

Most of this edition of NASSP is devoted to student discipline. Included are: "Strategies in Classroom Management," "Can Schools Cope with the Chronically Disruptive Student?" "Tips for a Student Discipline Program," "How Effective Are Their Strategies to Discipline?" "Self-Concept Continuum for Understanding Student Behavior," "Effective Communication: The Key to Student Management," "Dis-cipline and Classroom Management: Different Strokes for Different Folks," "Misbehavior: Challenging, Coping with the Classroom System," "Solving Behavior Problems by Changing the Environment," "Male/Female Dynamics and Student Discipline," "Focus on Discipline: An Inservice Program," "On-Campus Suspension: What It Is and Why It Works," "Positive Discipline: A Practical Approach to Disruptive Student Behavior."

292. Order in the Classroom! Postman, Neil. *Atlantic.* v244, n3, p35–38, Sep 1979.

The author affirms the importance of the classroom as a special place, aloof from the biases and techniques of the media; a place in which the uses of the intellect are given prominence in a setting of elevated language, civilized manners, and respect for social symbols. He insists that the classroom is a valid educational tool and students can and should learn to adapt their behavior to it.

293. Organizational Context of School Discipline: Analytic Models and Policy Options. Chesler, Mark et al. *Education and Urban Society.* v11, n4, p496–510, Aug 1979.

Five questions help frame this discussion of school discipline, discipline policies, and policy alternatives: what are the purposes of discipline policies; who determines discipline policies; what is the context of discipline policies; how is discipline policy implemented; and what is the political-educational context of discipline policy?

294. Responding to Student Misbehavior. Gorton, Richard A. *NASSP Bulletin.* v61, n405, p18–26, Jan 1977.

Nonpunitive approaches to discipline (changing the student, remediating learning problems, changing the school environment, and implementing alternative programs) can eventually reduce student misbehavior and should be considered as alternatives to punitive approaches for working with students who are discipline problems.

295. Secondary Discipline—Where Do Your People Come From? Jacob, Bob; Studer, Joe. *Thrust for Education Leadership.* v6, n5, p16–17,19, May 1977.

The fundamentals of sound secondary student discipline are embodied in six concepts. Suggests that recognition of these concepts and an enthusiastic effort to implement them will have a positive impact on the school.

296. Secondary Schools and Student Responsibility. Johnson, Christopher. *Phi Delta Kappan.* v59, n5, p338–41, Jan 1978 (EJ 169 848; Reprint: UMI).

Students must accept responsibility for their behavior—the blame for disciplinary failures should lie with the students who behave irresponsibly rather than with teachers, administrators, and parents. Control disappears as an overwhelming problem when students are given learning and behavioral responsibility.

297. Should Methods to Deal with Student Discipline Be Negotiated with Teacher Organizations? A Management Perspective. Metzler, John H.; Gerrard, Stanley C. *Journal of Law and Education.* v6, n1, p65–73, Jan 1977.

The author contends that the issue of student discipline is an important local problem and cannot be resolved by a futile and misguided attempt to negotiate it. Negotiations will only exacerbate the seeking and finding of a solution.

298. Should Methods to Deal with Student Discipline Be Negotiated with Teacher Organizations? The NEA Perspective. Dunlop, John E. *Journal of Law and Education.* v6, n1, p75–87, Jan 1977.

This article surveys current teacher organization bargaining efforts in the area of student discipline; covers the scope of teacher responsibilities in controlling disruptive student behavior, teacher concerns arising out of such responsibilities, and the extent to which collective bargaining has been utilized by teachers as a means for dealing with disruptive student behavior.

299. Solution to Discipline Problems in Schools. Hood, J. M. *Education.* v99, n4, p375–77, Sum 1979.

Described is a plan to reduce the dependence of teachers on school administrators as disciplinarians.

300. Some Principles for Secondary School Principals. Valenti, Ronald D. *NASSP Bulletin.* v61, n406, p91–93, Feb 1977.

Outlines basic management principles intended to aid secondary school principals in dealing with school discipline problems.

301. Successful School Suspension Programs: The Counselor's Role. Nielsen, Linda. *School Counselor.* v26, n5, p325–33, May 1979 (EJ 204 225; Reprint: UMI).

Despite the obstacles encountered in establishing the eight in-school suspension centers, the benefits for students were overwhelmingly positive. It is hoped that the specific suggestions formulated here can help counselors sponsor effective in-school suspension centers in their own schools.

302. Taking Charge of Student Behavior. Canter, Lee. *National Elementary Principal.* v58, n4, p33–36, 41, Jun 1979 (EJ 203 097; Reprint: UMI).

Describes and gives examples of the assertive discipline program. Also includes guidelines for an effective discipline plan.

303. *Today's Education.* v68, n2, p20–30, Apr-May 1979.

A special feature on discipline offers several articles on the topic: one deals with the dilemma of an authoritarian v a humanistic approach to discipline; another deals with deciding what level of teacher involvement in discipline will produce the best result; the last deals with the pros and cons of negotiating student discipline policy through collective bargaining.

304. Toughness: The Answer to Discipline Problems. Johnson, Arthur C. *NASSP Bulletin.* v63, n427, p130–31, May 1979.

The author states that we all know that students must get a good education, and discipline problems are the primary obstacle to this goal. Therefore, school administrators must eliminate this obstacle, and there is nothing short of an administratively tough regime that will produce the desired results.

305. Using the Rehabilitative Disciplinary Process. Moyer, David H. *NASSP Bulletin.* v63, n424, p1–7, Feb 1979 (EJ 196 049; Reprint: UMI).

The rehabilitative disciplinary process is the implementation of program variables that will have positive effects on the aggressive behavior pattern. This involves manipulation of environmental variables, peer relationships, teacher behavior, and productive behavior opportunities.

306. Usual but Not Cruel: Policy Guidelines on Corporal Punishment. Simpson, Robert J.; Dee, Paul O. *NOLPE School Law Journal.* v7, n2, p183–93, 1977 (EJ 183 292; Reprint: UMI).

Citing case law, this article attempts to provide public school districts with some guidelines if they opt to have paddling as one disciplinary technique available to the faculty. No philosophical presentation on the merits of corporal punishment is provided.

REPORTS

307. Absences. A Model Policy and Rules. Bartlett, Larry et al., Iowa State Department of Public Instruction, Des Moines, IA, Sep 1978, 17p; Appendix A may be marginally legible (ED 162 433; Reprint: EDRS).

The model attendance policy offered for consideration here suggests that school districts should encourage regular school attendance and may demand reasonable excuses for absences. Unexcused absences may warrant disciplinary action. The suggested rules that apply the attendance policy to specific situations cover a number of areas. A broad statement of attendance philosophy might introduce attendance rules. The rules may stipulate that after prolonged absences, parents may be contacted by the school. Rules concerning tardiness should be included in the attendance rules. Legitimate reasons for excusing absences should be clearly listed along with mechanisms for obtaining special permission to be absent. The rules for completing missed school work may be included. Penalties for unexcused absences might be probation, detention, or suspension. It is suggested that reduction of grades not be used as a disciplinary procedure. The duties and jurisdiction of the truancy officer may be incorporated in the attendance policy. These rules and policies should not be adopted verbatim, but rather adapted to individual situations and needs. The appendix includes Iowa laws concerning school attendance and cities studies on absenteeism and achievement.

308. Challenge for the Third Century: Education In a Safe Environment—Final Report on the Nature and Prevention of School Violence and Vandalism. Report of the Subcommittee to Investigate Juvenile Deliquency. 95th Congress, 1st Session. Committee Print. Bayh, Birch, Congress of the US, Washington, DC, Senate Committee on the Judiciary, Feb 1977, 102p (ED 135 091; Reprint: EDRS; also available from Superintendent of Documents, US Government Printing Office, Washington, DC 20402; Report No. 79-297-0).

This final report is designed to present a concise and practical overview of violence and vandalism with a particular emphasis on some of the factors underlying these problems and the various strategies that may be helpful in mitigating them. The report is intended primarily for the administrators, students, teachers, parents, and school staff that constitute the educational community and, accordingly, the various strategies suggested are school-based and educationally oriented. The report is divided into six sections. The first section is a concise overview of the extent of school related violence and vandalism in the nation. The second discusses several of the factors influencing the nature and development of these problems, including intruders, disciplinary and suspension policies, learning disabilities, truancy, and school size. The third section sets out the various strategies and models useful to schools in reducing violence and and vandalism. The fourth contains a series of suggested initiatives that the community may undertake to help implement the strategies discussed in the previous section. Section five presents a summary of the findings and recommendations of the report. The final section presents a list of suggested readings and a bibliography.

309. Climate for Learning: A Symposium. Creating a Climate for Learning, and the Humanizing Process. The Principal and School Discipline. *Curriculum Bulletin.* XXXII, 341. Johnson, Simon O.; Chaky, June, American Nepal Education Foundation, Oceanside, OR, Sep 1978, 24p (ED 161 142; Reprint: EDRS—HC not available; also available from Curriculum Bulletin, Oceanside, OR 97134).

This publication contains two articles focusing on creating a climate for learning. In "Creating a climate for Learning, and the Humanizing Process," Simon O. Johnson offers practical suggestions for creating a humanistic learning environment. The author begins by defining the basic concepts—humanism, affective education, affective situation, cognitive education, self-concept, and discipline. He then offers a number of practical suggestions on adopting humanistic principles, humanizing student goals and objectives, evaluating students, using humanistic teaching methods, and developing humanistic teacher characteristics. He also offers suggestions for improving the teacher-principal relationship. The author concludes with plans for making two specific humanistic school changes. In "The Principal and School Discipline," Johnson and June Chaky present and explain several suggestions emerging from their survey of over 700 teachers and administrators, incluing: (1) the principal should be a leader in staff development activities to give teachers the knowledge necessary to avoid classroom problems; (2) teacher evaluation should be a nonthreatening process that avoids the distrust out of which discipline problems spring; (3) the principal should ensure that fair rules and regulations are developed and enforced firmly; (4) the principal should make an effort to get to know pupils; and (5) discipline should be applied with tolerance and in the absence of confrontation.

310. Designing a Positive In-School Suspension Program. Mizell, M. Hayes, American Friends Service Committee, Jackson, MS, Southeastern Public Education Program, Oct 1977, 12p (ED 144 251; Reprint: EDRS).

This paper outlines the characteristics of an effective in-school suspension program designed to be a viable alternative to traditional out-of-school suspension for student misbehavior. The author emphasizes that an in-school suspension program must rest on a solid philosophical foundation which allows for defining and dealing with the root problems of misbehavior, not merely with the symptoms of discipline problems. Teachers and administrators must be willing to acknowledge that sometimes they contribute to student misbehavior. When instituting such a program, school personnel should give considerable attention to the process by which students are assigned to the program, how long they should stay, and to the process for follow-up once they leave. Special attention should be paid to academic difficulties, since frequently such difficulties underlie student discipline problems. Program personnel (counselors, teachers, aids) should be carefully selected, and the program should be evaluated at regular intervals throughout the school year.

311. Discipline, Corporal Pubishment, and Suspension. Garza, Gonzalo. Apr 1976, 13p; Paper presented at the Annual Meeting of the National School Boards Association (36th, San Francisco, CA, April 10–13, 1976) (ED 123 727; Reprint: EDRS).

Discipline is a major problem in many schools and an important issue to parents and educators alike. Discipline is commonly defined as negative reinforcement—punishment—instead of leadership and good teaching. Its definition should be expanded to relate it to the overall purposes of education. Discipline policy should be integrated with curriculum and instructional programs. Corporal punishment and suspension both have a place in the school discipline policy. The school's philosophy governing these two measures should be clearly stated in writing and made available to all interested parties. A coherent, comprehensive discipline policy to ease racial tensions is especially necessary in newly integrated schools.

312. Discipline in Schools: A Source Book. North Carolina State Department of Public Instruction, Raleigh, NC, 1977, 266p; not available in hard copy due to marginal reproducibility of original (ED 149 427; Reprint: EDRS; also available from State Department of Public Instruction, Raleigh, NC 27602).

The problem of student discipline is approached by synthesizing much that is known about child development, interpersonal relationships, identity, self-image, and change into a philosophy for individual growth and self-fulfillment. Goals, and methods for achieving them, are suggested that would help prevent discipline problems. These are to help each student to feel worthwhile, make the school experience more interesting, make and enforce more effective rules, involve parents, and provide effective security. Specific techniques and programs are presented for dealing with discipline problems when they do occur. Bariers are described which block school personnel from making constructive changes needed in order to solve school discipline problems, including unwritten rules; fear of change; and lack of money,

time, authority, and knowledge. Suggestions are offered for overcoming each barrier. The final sections contain a discussion of legal aspects and appendixes with an annotated bibliography, footnotes, and the questionnaire and a summary of ''A Study of Perceptions of Discipline Problems in Secondary Schools of North Carolina.''

313. Discipline in the Philadelphia Public Schools: A Working Document. Philadelphia School District, 1976, 63p (ED 132 710; Reprint: EDRS).

The purpose of the policies proposed in this guide is to improve discipline in the classrooms of the Philadelphia Public Schools. The guidelines emphasize the importance of parent and student cooperation in maintaining a livable environment in the schools. Student and parent rights and responsibilities are listed. The roles played by the principal and the professional staff (specifically, the teachers) in the discipline process are outlined. Suggested courses of action for principals and staff members to take when confronted with disruptive situations are described, along with the legal constraints and obligations faced by the school staff. The volume also deals with corporal punishment (and advises that its use is very hazardous and dubious), suspension and alternatives to suspension, and emergency situation procedures.

314. Discipline #1 Problem in the Schools? 40 Positive, Preventive (Include Grade Level) Prescriptions for Those Who Care. . . . Olivero, James L., Association of California School Administrators, April 1977, 65p.

Although everyone agrees that a discipline problem exists today, parents and educators perceive the problem differently. The research on causes of misconduct loosely defines them as factors relating to 1) the home: child abuse, reduced psychological support of negativism from the family, home-school philosophical conflict; and 2) the school, through ill-defined school goals and curriculum, poor communications, centralized decision making, staff fears, and stress. There are many positive, preventative prescriptions available to help keep discipline matters from being so overwhelming that productivity and satisfaction are nearly impossible. The prescriptions are categorized under three umbrella concepts: logistics and materials, processes, programs. Samples of the prescriptions are: transactional analysis, cultural awareness, teacher effectiveness training (TET), art projects for school pride, adult volunteers, imaginative scheduling, and stroke notes.

315. Guidelines for School Discipline. Pennsylvania State Department of Education, Harrisburg, PA, Oct 1976, 22p; Prepared by the Commisioner's Task Force on Student Responsibility and Discipline (ED 144 247; Reprint: EDRS).

These guidelines represent the partial completion of the first phase of a three-phase comprehensive study of discipline in the schools of Pennsylvania. In preparing this document, the state Task Force on Student Responsibility and Discipline attempted to present a practical, reasoned approach to the complex issue of student conduct and to provide clear direction for schools as they deal on a daily basis with the difficult problem of student discipline. The task force outlines a four-level student misconduct/disciplinary response structure intended to serve as a basis for discipline policies in Pennsylvania schools. The four levels classify student misbehavior ranging from minor misconduct, such as tardiness, through acts which result in violence to another person or to property, or which pose a direct threat to the safety of others. The suggested procedures and disciplinary options are geared to match the seriousness of each incident of misbehavior. The task force emphasizes that these guidelines should be tailored to characteristics and needs of each individual school. It also includes an examination of some major disciplinary issues, such as the use of suspension, and makes appropriate recommendations.

316. Improving Discipline in our Schools. An Operational Handbook for School Discipline Committees. Barbadora, Bernard, Comp. et al., Cincinnati Public Schools, OH, Department of Human Resources, Sep 1977, 63p; not available in paper copy due to marginal legibility of parts of original document (ED 165 260; Reprint: EDRS; also available from Cincinnati Public Schools, Department of Student Services, 230 East 9th Street, Cincinnati, OH 45202).

Board of Education Action Motion No. 16 requires each school in the Cincinnati system to establish a discipline committee to establish a formal structure designed to encourage cooperative efforts between and among staff, students, parents, and other concerned citizens. The focus of these cooperative efforts is to improve pupil behavior. This document has been developed as a general resource for school discipline committees and offers many how-to-do-it suggestions to help local committees work through the organization, planning, and evaluation processes. This information is, however, in no way meant to be all-inclusive. Suggested sources of resources for program development are included, as are several appendices providing background information on board policy; administrative procedures on suspension, expulsion, and removal from school; and related information.

317. Recommended Guide to Students' Rights and Responsibilities in Michigan. Michigan State Department of Education, Lansing, MI, 1974, 40p; not available in hard copy due to marginal legibility original document (ED 106 981; Reprint: EDRS).

These guidelines describe areas of concern as indicated by recent litigation, questions received from local school districts, and complaints received from parents and students. They also present, as a frame of reference, the status of current school law where and as it applies to the area of students' rights and responsibilities. The document is divided into five major sections: (1) background information and the purpose and need for such a document, (2) aspects of current law and practices relative to student behavior, (3) specific student behavior in terms of rights and responsibilities, (4) suspension of students along with guidelines for procedural due process, and (5) summary of the document with requests for continual review and reevaluation.

318. A Resource Manual for Reducing Conflict and Violence in California Schools. Pritchard, Ruth, Ed; Wedra, Virginia, Ed., California School Boards Association, Sacramento, 1975, 65p (ED 108 334; Reprint: EDRS—HC not available; also available from California School Boards Association, 800 Ninth Street, Sacramento, CA 95814).

This booklet was prepared to assist school administrators in developing effective strategies to cope with school violence and vandalism. Various chapters prepared by different authors address different perspectives and aspects of the problem. Topics of the chapters include early prevention, the interagency team concept, management in a team structure, parent education, a plan for school/agency/community cooperation, programs that are working, and security measures for vandalism and violence control. The final three sections describe two interagency youth service programs, examine the 1974 California law that created the School Attendance Review Board, and present a bibliography of publications and audiovisual materials dealing with school violence and youth service programs.

319. The School Principal and the Use of Detention, Suspension and Expulsion as Disciplinary Measures. Carter, David G. Apr 1976, 20p; Paper presented at the Annual Meeting of the American Educational Research Association (San Francisco, CA, April 19–23, 1976) (ED 122 382; Reprint: EDRS).

In discussing school discipline, the place to begin is by considering whether detention, suspension, and expulsion help students and resolve discipline problems. Detention seems to be most effective when the student is detained on the same day and as close as possible to the time the offense occurs, but too often detention is used merely as a "dumping tour." The rationale for suspension is that it serves as a mechanism for getting parents into the school; however, a survey by the Children's Defense Fund raises serious doubts about its effectiveness in that regard. There seems to be a growing trend among educators in favor of inschool discipline programs in place of suspension or expulsion. In working to resolve school discipline problems, the principal should utilize group processes that allow each member of the school organization to share in the necessary leadership. The principal sets the tone of discipline in the school. Every effort should be made to gain staff awareness and cooperation on discipline. The principal should act mainly as a catalyst for improving discipline. Once the proper disciplinary climate has been established, it becomes the principal's function to maintain that climate.

320. Student Conduct and Discipline. Minimum Standards. Oregon Administrative Rules 581-21-050 through 581-21-075. Adopted by the State Board of Education May 12, 1972, Oregon State Department of Education, Salem, OR, 1977, 14p (ED 141 930; Reprint: EDRS).

These suggested guidelines and model codes for student conduct and discipline represent an update of 1972 minimum standards in keeping with current statutes and court decisions. The Oregon State Board of Education published this document to provide guidance to local school districts in formulating discipline policies. The state standards listed here lay the groundwork for enforceable local rules of student conduct and discipline that will stand up to challenge in court. The state board emphasizes that once school districts adopt these guidelines they must follow them conscientiously. This document contains model codes relating to assembly of students, dress and grooming, the use of tobacco, corporal punishment, student records, and suspension and expulsion. The text of Oregon statutes and administrative rules pertaining to standards of student conduct are also included.

321. Students' Rights and Discipline. Ladd, Edward T.; Walden, John C. National Association of Elementary School Principals, Washington, DC, 1975, 74p (ED 109 773; Reprint: EDRS—HC not available; also available from National Association of Elementary School Principals, 1801 North Moore Street, Arlington, VA 22209, Stock No. 181-05616).

This book is meant to be practical. It attempts to clarify what one should keep in mind and to describe what courses of action are open when one confronts a particular situation. It is stated that teachers and principals encounter discipline problems not because they are deficient in skill or in virtue, but because they have inherited misleading definitions of their respective roles. What schools must do, may do, and may not do about disciplining is a matter of the governing of children. Individual chapters deal with the legal bases for student governance; fundamentals of governance—definitions, norms, and influence measures; the application of norms and compliance devices to different situations; the principal's leadership role in the governance program; governance tasks that trouble teachers and how principals can help; the ways to talk with students when there has been trouble; major offenses; and some considerations in building a governance

program. The appendixes provide a list of students' rights, a suggested list of important elemental norms for public elementary schools, and a list of basic influence procedures.

BOOKS

322. Codes of Student Discipline and Student Rights. Doob, Heather Sidor. Arlington, VA: Educational Research Service, Inc., 1975, 41p.

This work is intended to serve school administrators by providing basic information, positive suggestions, and examples pertaining to student codes. It presents findings of a recent inquiry regarding written codes of student discipline and replicates examples of selected codes. Seventy-six percent of the 538 responding school systems indicated that they have developed written codes of discipline for secondary level pupils. Large districts (enrollments of 25,000 or more) were the most likely to have such codes; very small districts (enrollments of 200-2,999), were the least likely. Written codes of student rights were much less prevalent; 34 percent of all respondents reported having a written code of student rights. The examples of written codes of student discipline and rights were drawn from the codes of school districts in ten different states.

323. Discipline or Disaster? Fastback Series, No. 8. Stoops, Emery; King-Stoops, Joyce. Bloomington, IN: Phi Delta Kappa, 1975, 38p.

Before discussing discipline policies and practices specifically, the authors survey the basis for discipline, the kinds of discipline, the needs and sources of discipline, and the relationships between parents and students and discipline. The authors point out the need for encouraging self-discipline and make the point that discipline and punishment are not the same thing. The bulk of the book discusses and provides examples of discipline policies on the district, building, and classroom levels. The discussion of classroom discipline provides general tips on classroom control, an analysis of problem types and problem situations, and suggestions for establishing classroom standards.

324. A Guide to Effective Secondary School Discipline: Manual for the New Administrator. Operations Notebook #24. Stammerjohan, Bob et al. Burlingame, CA: Association of California School Administrators, 1979, 34p.

This notebook is designed to serve as an operations manual for school administrators who are responsible for student discipline in public secondary schools. It is primarily intended as a primer for new administrators, but it can also provide valuable assistance to experienced administrators in dealing effectively with student discipline problems.

325. Maintaining Productive Student Behavior.
Swick, Kevin J. Washington, DC: National Education Association, 1977, 39p.

One evident point that emerges from a look at the current status of the behavior problem in our schools is the varying and sometimes confusing solutions that are put forth to solve the problem. What is needed is an examination of the problem from the perspective of a research and application process within each school-community setting. The emotional debate over how to bring about productive behavior among students usually leads to the polarization of attitudes among those conducting the debate.

The author attempts to clarify the status of constructive and destructive behavior through a study of professional literature and research studies. Utilizing this literature survey as a base, he provides some ideas on how educators can begin to develop a logical and orderly examination of the problem in their own district or school situation. The remaining chapters are an attempt toward clarifying, organizing, and implementing a process by which professional and lay personnel can begin to examine disruptive behavior in their local settings and, hopefully, to initiate some useful procedures to improve their particular educational climates.

326. Report: Discipline in Our Big City Schools.
Washington, DC: National School Boards Association, 1977, 45p.

The National School Boards Association Discipline Committee found that discipline-related problems are increasing in frequency and have become a major concern to school authorities. The committee surveyed more than 100 school districts throughout the United States, concentrating on large urban districts. On the basis of the data it collected, the committee made six recommendations: (1) Districts should establish task forces to collect information on discipline problems; (2) students, parents, teachers, and administrators should be involved when discipline policies are developed; (3) discipline policies should be written and distributed to all interested parties; (4) teachers should be offered inservice training to learn to deal with student offenders consistently and fairly; (5) school employees should be encouraged to exercise their legal rights to prevent violence in the schools; and (6) alternatives to suspension and alternative educational programs should be set up. This report also includes sample discipline policies from various school districts.

327. School Discipline Desk Book. Howard, Eugene R. West Nyack, NY: Parker Publishing Co., Inc., 1978, 250p.

The author of this handbook maintains that substantial school improvement can take place only within an orderly environment. To achieve a positive educational climate, he lists numerous suggestions to handle school discipline problems. Individual chapters cover conducting a campaign against crime and violence, handling discipline problems

effectively, helping teachers reduce discipline problems, unrigging the school (including improving students' self-concepts), increasing student involvement in school activities, and improving student morale by modifying the curriculum. Two successful discipline improvement programs, one in an urban high school and one in an elementary school, are described in detail. An annotated bibliography is appended.

328. Student Discipline: Practical Approaches (National School Boards Association Research Report 1979–2). Washington, DC: National School Boards Association, 1979, 29p.

This report covers trends in discipline policies and policymaking and alternative and innovative school programs designed to diminish behavioral problems in the classroom. The programs range from improvements in a school's physical plant to specific action plans for teachers and options in the curriculum designed to stimulate alienated students. Some of the programs assembled in this report are preventive; others serve as intervention measures.

329. Violence in Our Schools: What to Know about It—What to Do about It. Columbia, MD: National Committee for Citizens in Education, 1975, 52p.

This handbook for parents and citizens does not emphasize assessment of the scope of violence in the schools so much as it emphasizes the way in which parents and citizens can better understand the many factors that create the problem and may lead to its modification. The handbook begins by examining how citizens can become involved in the schools, what they need to know, and who—teachers, students, community members, and the people who take care of the building—must be involved in a school security plan. The handbook goes on to discuss the training of security people, the physical plant, equipment, the educational program, school policies, discipline, and implementation of the security plan. Extensive appendixes cover a wide range of information related to violence in the schools, including results of a survey on the extent of violence in the schools, recent Supreme Court decisions on student rights, and sources of further information.

Index